HAVE YOU SEEN THE GLORIES?
Walking in the golden land

JOHN FOWLER

HAVE YOU SEEN THE GLORIES?
Walking in the golden land

JOCK'S HILL PRESS
Linlithgow, Scotland

HAVE YOU SEEN THE GLORIES?

First published in Great Britain in 1999
by JOCK'S HILL PRESS
15 Jock's Hill Crescent, Linlithgow,
West Lothian EH49 7BJ Scotland

Design by Roy Petrie

British Library Cataloguing Publication Data
Have You Seen the Glories? Walking in the golden land
1 Travel
2 Walking
ISBN 1 902442 00 8
Printed in Great Britain by INTERPRESS
8 Huntershill Road, Bishopbriggs, Glasgow G64 1RH

Some passages in this book draw on articles written for
The Herald newspaper

for Mary

The climb's done
　　　　free now
you walk a far land's trackless hills

One day on Stob Binnein

we climbed through mist and rain
into an upper world of clear blue sky.
The surrounding peaks jutted out
like islands in a sea of white cloud
on which the sun cast our shadows,
ghostly and unreal, ringed by rainbow haloes.
When we descended back into the gloom
we met another walker.
Her eyes shone with excitement
as she asked: 'Did you see the glories?'

CONTENTS

Part One

CELTIC
fringes

1

Dreams and follies

When I was a boy growing up at the seaside the nearest mountains were twenty miles away across the Firth of Clyde. From my bedroom window I'd see fiery sunsets over Goat Fell and the Arran peaks, a jaggy stencil on the skyline.

I remember a poem from boyhood. Daydreaming at my battered wooden schooldesk with the sun shining mockingly outside, I became aware of teacher speaking W J Turner's poem Romance

> *When I was but thirteen or so*
> *I went into a golden land,*
> *Chimborazo, Cotopaxi*
> *took me by the hand . . .*

I sat up, I listened

> *I stood where Popocatapetl*
> *in the sunlight gleams*

I stood there too, in fancy. But where were Chimborazo, Cotopaxi, Popocatapetl? I knew nothing of these mountains with exotic names and the Andes meant no more to me than a brown curl on the map. It didn't occur to me that people might want to climb them.

I knew people climbed in the Alps. We had an English reader which contained an extract from Edward Whymper's Scrambles Amongst the Alps (and particularly, on the Matterhorn): 'The rope broke . . . We saw our unfortunate companions sliding down on their backs . . . They disappeared one by one, and fell from precipice to precipice'. Gulp! In the same class our teacher (maybe that balding, tubby little man at the blackboard was a walker himself) talked with enthusiasm about the climber and mountain photographer Frank Smythe. Something must have stuck. Many years later I came across Smythe's books and read them eagerly.

The distant and unattainable is always fascinating. Some time ago as a journalist I happened to be in Tbilisi in Georgia. My hotel bedroom was on the top floor of a high building and the lift was slow in coming. As I waited I glanced out of the window. Far away, a hundred miles perhaps, the dark cone of a distant mountain stood out against the sky.

I knew it instantly, though I'd never seen it before. The previous day on a visit to a cliffside monastery in the Georgian foothills I'd seen a painting with a pale saint in blue in the foreground and, in the background, that very snow-covered mountain. The likeness was unmistakable. Almost as I looked, the strange mountain dissolved in the haze of the advancing morning, and for the rest of the hot day, though I was always glancing at the horizon, it remained invisible. But in the evening as I sat with friends in the hotel restaurant it came into view again, a thin, black silhouette against red sky.

I realised that it must be Mount Kazbek, the second highest peak in the Caucusus (in fact in Europe – it's higher than Mont Blanc). I hoped for another sight of it but it didn't show again.

Mine have been lesser hills, and it was a long time before I climbed in earnest. The first casual effort ended in a blizzard on Ben Narnain. Narnain is one of the Arrochar Alps, the name popularly given to a cluster of rugged peaks at the head of Loch Long, within easy reach of Glasgow where I was a student. I'd never heard of Narnain and didn't know where it was when someone suggested a winter outing. None of us belonged to the university mountaineering club or had any reasonable gear – I remember walking in black tackety boots left over from National Service. Maybe someone had a map and compass and knew how to use them, but I doubt it.

We got off the bus at Arrochar and walked round the head of the loch, but the only detail that remains in memory is coming to a windswept halt in a bowl in the hills – possibly the big corrie at the top of the Sugach burn, or maybe even on the col below the final rise to Narnain – in a maelstrom of whirling snowflakes, where we wisely opted for a return to safer ground. We descended, bedraggled, to sea level and the comfort of a blazing fire in the nearest hotel, where we attempted to dry off steaming clothes, warmed our frozen fingers and swallowed a dram or two. There was never any more talk of hill-walking among residents of Kelvin Lodge. We resumed normal pursuits, which meant playing 78s on the battered gramophone in the lounge (Tommy Dorsey's Sentimental Trumpet and Solomon playing the Emperor Concerto, etc), the occasional bout of study, and girls.

One of the Narnain adventurers lived in the Lake District and took me over Helvellyn's Striding Edge in thick mist. Walking blind, it didn't seem at all scary. Later I got in tow with Holiday Fellowship (now simply the HF) and on one of their outings climbed Ben Lui in the wet and saw nothing at the top but a few shadowy figures among damp boulders (mountaineering without the view is an easily acquired habit). One of the HF regulars was a stocky wee man in his seventies – it seemed a great age to me at the time – one of those tough old hikers who go on for ever. He'd been a pharmacist and had started a post-grad course in biology which involved trips to Dublin to study the stomach contents of a body preserved in the bog since the Middle Ages. We received regular reports on what the seeds and stuff lodged in his gut revealed about his lifestyle.

My own lifestyle changed and hill-walking stopped for several years until a chance meeting in the bar of the Ubiquitous Chip set it on course again, if with a stagger. The Chip is a Glasgow restaurant famed for its cobbled courtyard and hanging plants, the haunt of business lunchers. The upstairs bar, a low-ceilinged smoky place (does the whiff of toilets still linger on the stairs, I wonder?), was the watering place for broadcasters, literati, and West Enders in general. It was there that one or two scratch outings were arranged, including an ill-fated attempt on Cruachan.

The several peaks of Ben Cruachan, crushed together like a

row of bad teeth, make a fine jagged crest above Loch Awe. Four of us set out to conquer it. One of our number was super-fit, ran marathons and worked in winter as a guide for the British Ski Club in the Alps, and she offered to take the lead – said she knew the hill (she'd been on it once before in bright sunshine). For this expedition we used Poucher – W. A. Poucher's tubby little book The Scottish Peaks, illustrated by his own black and white photographs on which a straggly white line is superimposed to indicate the route. We went wrong from the start, lured into a detour by a line of old signposts leaning at drunken angles and pointing to a destination unknown, because illegible. The hilltops were enveloped in mist and the higher ground boulder-strewn. When we emerged on the ridge we were aware of higher slopes looming above. A solitary man wearing a bunnet and smoking a pipe strolled by. Where were we? He didn't know either, but wasn't at all rattled, puffing sagely on his pipe and walking on. At least he had the sense to follow the ridge while we, foolishly, started a descent on the other side. It soon steepened dangerously. The wet ground was a mix of grass and loosely bedded rock and we had to claw our way carefully with every step. Finally one of us – not I – restored sanity by insisting we retrace our steps.

It wasn't easy. We had to clamber, and on the way someone dislodged a lump of rock which skimmed past my left shoulder and disappeared into the grey void, its fall marked by a succession of sickening bumps and thumps. Later I tried to calculate where we'd been, and came to the conclusion that we'd started to descend a corrie wall which becomes almost precipitous. Even if we'd got down unscathed it would have been in a sombre glen far from any road or habitation. Most likely we'd have had to spend a night in the open. We'd got away with it, but only just. Something clearly had to be done.

From their home in a cottage near Stirling two women started a business leading guided walks. They called their operation C-N-Do ('see and do' if you like) and it's since grown considerably. But I knew it in the early days when it was just the two of them. Margaret, who had captained the Scottish women's fencing team, and Dorothy, a post-graduate student of biotechnology, met at university and decided to turn their yen for the outdoors into a career. To begin with I went out with C-N-Do quite a lot. It was a good way to get to know the hills and how to find my way around them, and I liked the company.

Four days in Knoydart introduced me to a wild stretch of country and the dubious pleasures of sleeping in bothies. All I knew about Knoydart was that it lay somewhere on the north-west coast and had been the scene of a famous land dispute in 1948 involving the Seven Men of Knoydart, when irate locals back from the war staked out claims on the vast sporting estate of an absentee landowner. Since then it had changed hands more than once, bits and pieces had been sold off, and there had been attempts to secure at least part of it in the public interest. The best development so far has been the acquisition of ground by the John Muir Trust, an organisation devoted to the conservation of wild country.

There were five of us; Margaret, myself, two girls and the Silent Man of Knoydart. Chris was a word miser, the most laconic man I've ever met. While the rest of us chattered he kept mum. He'd just walked the length of the West Highland Way and possibly he'd exhausted his stock of conversation en route. I think I got about a hundred words out of him altogether, and most of them were monosyllables.

There are huge hills in Knoydart but that trip took us over passes rather than tops. The first night we spent at A'Chuill bothy, which was bare but had a fireplace, and the first task was to comb the bog land round about in search of old tree roots to burn. The Highlands are mainly a treeless landscape now but the peat bogs offer an apparently inexhaustible supply of these preserved remnants of the old forest. Next morning we crossed the Dessary burn by a rickety log bridge and headed for the pass of Mam na Cloiche-Airde by way of the limpid pools of Lochan a'Mhaim. The weather was clammy and I was tempted to skinny dip. I stripped and waded in cautiously, but the pool was icy and before the water reached my knees my courage failed. Two other walkers appeared and joined us at the side of the lochan, one of whom pulled out a telescopic fishing rod, and before long the trout were leaping on to his hooks. That night we encountered them again at Sourlies bothy on the shore of Loch Nevis, where the little one fried trout in butter for their dinner. It smelt delicious (we made do with packets and tins). It transpired he was a chef on a North Sea oil platform. They had worked out the perfect partnership: the tall one caught the fish and the wee one cooked them. Oddly enough, I met another North Sea chef in a youth hostel in Torridon not long after. He brought his own knives and pans. He was the wonder of the company the night he drummed up beef teryaki followed by crêpes suzettes, flambéd of course. Flames leaped from the frying pan. Not many people can have sampled cordon bleu in a youth hostel kitchen.

The following day we walked across the sands, searched for an ancient cemetery on the foreshore, climbed through our obligatory pass and descended by way of Gleann Unndalain, stopping to gather firewood from among the few trees struggling to exist in a narrow gorge. Then, bundles under our arms and boughs over our shoulders, we trudged over the machair to the bothy at Barisdale, where the fire, once lit, proved a smoking monster. Only those with cast-iron lungs and leather tear ducts managed to relax in the blue-black haze that thickened in the tiny building. Most of us spent the evening lounging by the open door and some preferred to camp out on the machair, where the air was sweet.

We had an early start in order to catch the Mallaig ferry at Inverie. It was wet all the way from sea level to the 1,300-foot pass at Mam Barisdale, and then followed a wearisome tramp for miles down the glen. We trooped into the hotel at Inverie just as the hands on the clock in the bar reached half-past two. 'Sorry, we're closed', said the young woman as she mopped slops from the bar. So much for Highland hospitality. Five minutes later a gang of locals burst in demanding pints, and got them. 'We're open again', she remarked brightly to the world in general. But by that time we weren't interested – we were drinking tea.

I had another few days with C-N-Do when we climbed Liatach, Beinn Eighe and Beinn Alligin, three great mountains in Torridon. It was good to be with company, but I was getting restive. I wanted to strike out on my own.

2

Purple mountain, misty hill

Soft is the word. Soft, say the Irish by way of a greeting on a mild morning when a thin rain drifts gently 'like a brush of dew on the cheek', as Tim Magennis put it as we enjoyed the crack in a Dublin pub. Tim was telling me about weather lore and local custom. He knew about all weathers because he'd voyaged round the world under sail. Apart from that, he was a good man to meet just then because he worked for the Irish Tourist Board and I needed to know about the hills.

Tim introduced me to two marvellous elderly ladies who ran Parson's bookshop in Dublin, where I went to buy maps.

'This is Miss Flaherty', he said.

'O'Flaherty', she corrected him. He wasn't listening.

'How are you, Miss Flaherty?' he asked kindly.

Miss O'Flaherty was pleased to have a walker on her premises. Had she not herself climbed in the Himalayas when young? She was a game old gal.

Parson's was an institution in Dublin. It was small and poky. On the walls were photos of the Irish literati who had browsed there over the generations, among them William Butler Yeats and James Joyce. Books were stacked on the floor and jostled on the shelves in great disorder. I looked forward to revisiting it when next in Dublin but by that time it had gone. The books had been sold and the ladies were in retirement.

All my life I'd thought of Ireland as green and mainly flat and it came as a surprise to discover, scanning the atlas, that dotted all over the island were mountains that reached 3,000 feet and more. In places they rose from the very rim of the sea. They had strange names: Knockanaffrin, Knockaunabulloga, Knockaunpeebra, Knockavulloge, Knockmeadow – and that's just a few of the Knocks. There were others. McGillicuddy's Reeks were mountains and not just a whimsical name for a dance or a dish or what an Irishman wears under his breeks, and the Mountains of Mourne were no mere Guinness-fuelled fancy of a songster in a snug.

So I packed my new boots, a new compass (these were my early hill-climbing days) and Joss Lynam's book The Irish Peaks and took a flight in a big SAS plane that carried a sum total of me and four others to Dublin, where I hired a car and drove some two hundred miles to the west. Killarney was blessed as few other Irish highlands were; it had a one-inch map. Anyone used to walking with Ordnance Survey maps in Britain is in for a rude shock in Ireland – or was then, a few years ago, when the best on offer (even at Parson's) was likely to be a hopelessly inadequate half-inch series. Lynam's book is forthright on the subject: 'The scale is too small for them to be really suitable for the hill-walker . . . many minor and a few major physical features do not appear . . . the delineation of the crags and cliffs is arbitrary in the extreme'. I discovered the truth of this, to my cost.

(One morning that week I passed Joss Lynam's country cottage – or so three cheery women frying breakfast in a caravan informed me it was. They offered me a cup of tea and then opened a discussion on the state of northern Ireland, which I thought best not to get deeply involved in. My saving grace in their eyes was to be not English but a Scot.)

Day One dawned (or rather I woke to find it) soft. It was mild and the rain caressed my cheek. I took a chance and headed for Kate Kearney's Cottage (not a cottage at all but Kate Kearney's gift shop, restaurant and pub) at the mouth of the Dunloe Gap, on one side of which looms the Purple Mountain.

'Don't get lost up there', said the man at the last house before the hill. 'I don't want to have to look for you'.

By the time I got through the drenching bracken and the ankle-grabbing heather the mist was lifting. On the ridge a gale of wind hit me and I'd trouble keeping my feet, but in compensation there were broad views of the Killarney loughs and the saw-toothed ridge of the Reeks across the gorge. In late afternoon I descended to the narrow road that snakes through the Gap, where the tarmac was caked with horse dung and the air filled with the clip-clopping of hoofs and the rumbling of wheels, for the Gap is the route of a brisk pony and trap trade. Approaching the summit of the pass I found myself stuck behind a minor traffic jam, with a young couple in jaunting car drawn by an ambling pony ahead of a car and a mini-van. Neither vehicle could pass it. I followed at the tail end inhaling the exhaust fumes. I decided to take action, broke into a jogtrot and passed the lot, at which the pony took fright, tossed its little mane, kicked up its nimble heels and smartly rattled past me, followed by the car and the van. We were on the down grade by then; pony and trap, car and van drew away and I saw no more of them.

The small pub at Beaufort crossroads had a welcoming log fire blazing, and a loud American tourist leaning on the bar recalling the day Kennedy was shot.

'The worst day of my life', he said.

'It was indeed', concurred the big-bearded local on a stool beside him, gazing solemnly into his Guinness. Country Irish, I suspect, will always agree with Americans buying drinks.

I spent two nights at a house called Mountain View, though there was never a mountain that I could see from it. Perhaps there was a skylight affording the view. Three other guests arrived at the same time, two Dutch teenage girls and their grandfather who were on a cycling tour round Ireland. Rudo, the old man, though he was 78 looked as if he could outpace the girls. In youth, he said, he and his wife had been great hikers. They'd tramped all over Wales and the Lake District before the war, he'd climbed in the Alps, and he'd made expeditions beyond the Arctic Circle in Norway, including a spell of three days when it snowed without let and they'd had to navigate through the white-out by compass and dead reckoning. He was a tough old man.

Rudo and I rose early and fretted each morning at the non-appearance of breakfast. Meta, our landlady, was a charming and energetic woman who served good food (fresh salmon for dinner with a salad that had been growing in the garden half an hour before), but her concept of time was hazy and her meals were movable feasts, always later than you hoped.

'When would you like breakfast?' she asked.

Eight, I said, not wanting to be too demanding. We compromised at eight-thirty. The clock struck. Eight-thirty came and went, and nine, and at twenty past the bacon and eggs appeared at last on the table. So there was no early dash to the hills.

Progress was further hindered by a street fair in the little town of Killorglin where crowds thronging the bright stalls overflowed into the street and blocked the traffic. Cars, when able to move at all, had to inch forward at a snail's pace.

Then there was the cow. Cows are always a hazard on Irish roads, where herds of them are apt to wander at will, but this was a lone beast in a lane leading to Coomasaharn Lake. She stood under a high hedge pendent with red fuschia blossom, munching sweet clover at the verge. Her dung-caked backside stuck out into the middle of the road. There wasn't room to drive past and nothing would budge her. When she ambled off at a stately trot, fat belly gently swinging under her, she kept to the crown of the lane. I got out of the car, I shouted, I shooed, I contemplated giving her encrusted rump a whack (but thought better of it, being a townie and not knowing the ways of beasts). So I sat at the wheel until sweet herbage in an adjoining field tempted her aside and I could edge past her buttocks.

I perched the car precariously on a patch of shelving ground above the lake, which lurks in a corrie (or coum in Irish terms) under a curtain of dark cliffs. The boulder-strewn slopes levelled out on to a grassy whaleback trenched by bog hags which were difficult to avoid and had me clambering in and out among pits of black peat. The top of Coomcamaree came as a disappointment, for there can hardly be a more insignificant mountain top. It is gently rounded, boggy and featureless, without even one stone raised on another to indicate the summit.

Coomcamaree is the highest point on a long horseshoe

which ends in a marked dip and a final knob. On reaching the end of the ridge I discovered that it was joined to the knob by a knife-edge ridge that fell away in steep scree slopes on either side, each terminating below in a small black lough. I consulted the book. An arête, it said.

I have a poor head for heights, and it was worse in those days. But there was no turning back. I gritted my teeth, fixed my gaze on my feet and the yard of narrow rock immediately ahead, and tried to shut out peripheral vision. I crouched (it seemed safer that way) and once I even dropped on my hands and knees. It was a shaming display and I'm glad there was no one to see it. Once I was on safe ground I took a deep breath, thought of a large whiskey in the nearest pub, sped from the dreadful place and didn't look back. I don't suppose the arête was so fearsome after all, and if I went back now I might find it pretty tame, but on that day I quaked.

The hill I most wanted to climb was Brandon, St Brendan's mountain, which goes plumb into the Atlantic on the Dingle peninsula, west of Tralee. But then it rained, and that rain could not be described as soft. It pelted. Fat raindrops stotted from the road. The windscreen wipers worked overtime. Grudgingly I turned back to the Slieve Mish mountains and the less ambitious Catherconree. (Commcamaree, Catherconree, how they sing, those Irish mountain names!)

Barber shop poles striped red and white marked the first stage of the route. Joss Lynam is withering in his contempt for this feature: 'The true mountaineer frowns on such aids, as they encourage the high-heel shoes and handbag brigade'. And he adds severely: 'Only those adequately clothed to withstand the sudden changes in weather conditions which are a feature of our hills, and equipped with map and compass – which they are able to use – should take to higher ground'. I had no handbag but I had a compass which I believed I could use, I had boots, cagoule and waterproof trousers and so I launched myself confidently into the mirk.

The barber poles ended some way up at an archaeological

feature, a prehistoric fort built of red boulders like an outsize drystane dyke. It was there that I met Wayne. Wayne was a young thickset man in oilskins over tweeds, with a check cap on his head. He was puffing on a pipe reflectively and leaning on a blackthorn stick, the picture of a man at peace with the world. I was surprised to learn that he was a farmer. The farming folk I've met on mountains tend to have business there, like shepherds. But Wayne had recently taken up hill walking. He was a little put out by the mist. Would I care to show him the way?

'Follow me', I said.

We reached the top of Catherconree and I suggested continuing a mile or so to an adjacent hill called Baurtreegaum. As contorted, tor-like eminences drifted in and out of the gloom – they all looked alike – my confidence slowly began to ebb. I was uneasily aware that I'd never used a compass in earnest before, and there seemed to be something odd about this one. Try as I might, I couldn't figure it out at all. Where the hell were we going? Lost, lost. In a little while my unease began to seep through to Wayne, waiting patiently while I crouched down over the instrument. 'We'll be all right, then?' he asked defensively. His voice had an edge which hadn't been there before.

As time passed I realised that we'd missed the summit and decided to retrace our steps. Unfortunately there was no sign of the ghostly tors to guide us back, and as one by one they failed to reappear I suggested losing height to see what we could see below the clouds. Once in the clear I sat on a boulder looking down a long and unfamiliar river valley to the sea, trying to place it on the map. Meanwhile Wayne started to get panicky and was all for heading in the wrong direction entirely. Opportunely, the mist lifted slightly, just enough for us to distinguish a shadowy figure on the skyline not very far away – and near him, a pole, one of the barber sort as it turned out when we came close. Nothing would stop Wayne now. He loped off at a brisk pace and when I caught up with him at the fort he proferred a limp hand and we parted more coolly than we'd met.

I puzzled over that compass. I knew in theory how to take a bearing, but somehow the thing in my hand didn't work the way the book said it should. In due course I discovered that the make I'd bought worked on a different principle from the more common Silva compass. It's a poor workman who blames his tools – but Wayne, you'd be safe with me now. Trust me.

The Irish jaunt was rounded off in perfect weather. Connemara and Mayo were bathed in sunshine and I enjoyed broad summit views to the Atlantic. All through the western arc a mosaic of islands merged into the haze of blue sea and sky. Pale golden beaches and fingers of sea etched the land's margin. It was hot and it was August – in fact it was August bank holiday, and that was a problem. Accommodation became difficult to find. There was no room at all for a man on his own in the B&Bs of Clifden, a small seaside resort near the tip of the Connemara peninsula. Clifden had the air of a miniature, primmer Blackpool without the tower, the trams and the lights. The smell of chip fat mingled with the reek of peat smoke (but at least it seemed to keep the midges at bay). The most exciting shop window display on the prom was a selection of hairy tweed hats and knobbly walking sticks.

No room either at the Alcock and Brown Hotel, the best in town, named after the transatlantic aviators who ditched in a nearby bog. But a helpful young man at the desk phoned around and booked me the last room in a lesser establishment. I went to sleep in a spartan cubicle tinted rose by the setting sun, and woke again on the stroke of midnight as a ceilidh began in the ballroom below. A few hundred guests were having bank holiday fun. The accordion crescendoed and the wailing notes of an uncertain trumpet curled into the night air. A child wailed in the next room. I even thought of getting up, dressing, and going down to join in.

When it was all over there were volleys of farewells and a noisy unlocking and locking of bedroom doors all along the corridor, then a further half-hour of sleeplessness to endure as empty beer kegs were clanked down the lane. Next day there were traffic jams on the way to Dublin races, and I nearly missed my plane.

3

A wake on the West Highland Line

When I lived in the centre of Glasgow in an old garment factory converted into flats I went to the hills by bus or train, as people had done in the old days (I was short of money at the time and hadn't a car). Two railway stations and a bus terminus were within ten minutes' walk.

You meet all sorts on the train. An Englishman in a tweed jacket on the train to Crianlarich told me he was a rancher on the Isle of Mull – of sheep, I learned. We got talking about wildlife and he said his gamekeeper had been 'treed' by a stag (ie chased up a tree). The keeper had been forced to flee from an angry stag in the rutting season and had to perch in the branches for several hours until the beast wearied and trotted off. But mainly the rancher talked of Frederick Courtney Selous, whose biography he was reading.

The book was entitled The Mighty Nimrod and the illustration on the front cover showed a white hunter sitting in a proud Anglo-Saxon attitude on a tree trunk with an assegai propped by his side and a hefty big-barrelled gun in his hands. The result of the chase was pictured on the back cover of the book; an elephant tumbling to its knees. Selous had been a great slaughterer of elephants in his day, when Britain ruled much of colonial Africa. The rancher explained that the antique weapon Selous cradled was a muzzle-loaded express which required skill and courage in use on the veldt. The hunter would ride close enough to the elephant to get in one disabling shot, then would turn and gallop away hell for leather, reloading as best he could while pursued by the wounded animal. It took a second shot to deliver the coup de grâce. We agreed that Selous, who took the tusks as trophies, wouldn't get away with it now. 'You wouldn't buy a pair of ivory brushes today', said the rancher.

Months later it felt like meeting an old friend when, browsing
at an antiquarian book sale, I picked up the Life of Frederick
Courtney Selous DSO. 'Killed in action 1917', said the caption to
the frontispiece, picturing him as a veteran subaltern with a grizzled
Jan Smuts beard. As I flicked through the pages my eye lighted on
the sentence:'In April 1906, Selous went all the way to Bosnia just
to take the nest and eggs of the Nutcracker'. Presumably there was
a window of peace in Bosnia that year. How fare its nutcrackers
now?

The rancher was heading for Oban and the boat to his isle,
and I left him at Tyndrum. I aimed to climb Ben Oss (more of Oss,
tiresome hill, later). Once on the well-trodden path through the
Cononish glen the solid mass of Ben Lui, neighbour of Oss, hove
into view, its summit blotted out by storm clouds. A blatter of sleet
and hail drove me for shelter behind a giant mound of cow dung
and straw at the side of the track, where I donned waterproofs.
Clouds were scudding across the sky at a fast rate and every so often
the rising wind would throw a lashing storm in my direction. I
reached snow and then ice and had to put on crampons. Higher up,
ribbons of powdery snow were being whipped across the flat back
of the ridge, and blown off in a fine smoke. The twin summits of
Ben Dubhchraig came curling beautifully into view in a patch of
sunshine, closer than Oss, but by now progress had to be hard
won. For every two steps I took forward I staggered back one. In
view of the black menace swirling round Lui and heading my way, I
aborted the climb.

The Inverey Inn in Tyndrum is welcome at such a
time. 'Look at the state of him', I heard a beer belly mutter to his
mates at the bar as I staggered in from the gale, tousled. A notice at
the bar advertised a farewell party for the miners that night, 9pm till
late. There's gold in them hills and exploratory digging on a seam
in Ben Chuirn had just come to a successful conclusion. It was only
five o'clock, but here, clearly, was a miners' advance party getting
primed for the hooly. A colonnade of empty pint glasses stood on
the bar in front of them. I imagined the shock of any unsuspecting

traveller who might drop in later for a quiet dram.

Paul was going to pray. Paul was a stocky man in his late sixties with pebble glasses on his nose. Outside the landscape was white with big slops of snow floating down from the sky, blanketing the earth and making white ropes of the tree branches. Paul had been reading a black-covered book and he wore a silver cross over his jersey. He'd been a priest (the name Paul was assumed on taking orders) and he was on his way to a retreat in Dalmally to say prayers for a dying friend. He'd been a medical missionary in Africa and spoke sorrowfully of poverty and disease on the continent, and of the corruption of the rich and powerful.

He was blind in one eye. It must have been a family weakness because his sister was blind in one eye too, only hers was the other one. She'd married a man who was blind in both eyes. I pictured the three of them together, husband in the middle and Paul and his sister keeping a lookout on either side. When I told this to Paul he laughed. He said it was amazing how little the blind man was handicapped.

I left the train at Tyndrum (prayers next stop). I started off on the main road along Strath Fillan towards the farm road-end at Auchtertyre. It was sleeting and two women with packs on their back trudged towards me, one about a hundred yards ahead of the other.

'How far is it to Tyndrum?' asked the younger one, in a despairing tone of voice.

We stopped to talk. They'd deserted the West Highland Way for the road, thinking the walking would be easier, and both were weary. The older woman looked exhausted. As she approached with dragging footsteps the younger one shouted with a touch of hysteria: 'He's going to climb the hill!' She thought I was daft.

I didn't climb much. It turned out to be a day of dither and flounder. Deep soft snow encased Gleann a'Clachain, the narrow valley into which I plodded with hope of climbing Ben Challum, a considerable mountain. I ploughed my way down to the river bank

where shielings, once a place of shelter for herdsmen but mere
heaps of stone now, were marked on the map – no sign of them
under the blanket of snow. The river wasn't running high but it was
broad and its stony bed looked slippery, and I was reluctant to
cross. Above, the long slopes leading to Challum were lost in mist
and the gullies choked with new snow. I lost heart and turned
away.

But the white wall at the head of the glen looked an
interesting alternative, capped by a lesser peak than Challum, but
not a hill to be slighted even if the writer and arch-Munroist
Hamish Brown dismisses it as undistinguished. But in the end Cam
Chreag too proved elusive. Progress through the snow-filled glen
was hot, wearisome and slow. I struggled to a large boulder warmed
by the sun on which I perched and ate a sandwich. A jet plane
roared overhead. I was nervous of avalanches. Could the noise of a
plane trigger one off? – I didn't know. The glen was narrow and I
felt vulnerable below steep slopes overloaded with new snow and
now exposed to the sun. Besides, time was shortening and Cam
Chreag still lay a couple of hours ahead. I turned again.

Not to return meekly by the way I'd come I diverted over a
ridge above Tyndrum, taking in a small eminence called Meall
Buidhe. A stiff wind drove stinging snow in my eyes as I came off
the top, making it difficult to pick out details in the
landscape. Clefts with massy headwalls of snow crossed my path and
had to be wallowed through and it was slow going to reach lower
ground.

The army passed me on the road. Two Land-Rovers roared
past, stopped at the station, and men in mottled battledress carrying
black guns leapt to the ground. They raced along the platform and
disappeared up the line. The drama was never explained. In due
course my train arrived, and I saw no more of the action.

One winter morning I rose early to catch the 5.50 Fort
William train. I expected it to be quiet – it always was. It would be
dark outside, the pale faces of the few sleepy passengers reflected in

the blank windows, and there'd be no view. If the heaters were working full blast as usual it would be stuffy and I'd nod off.

But that day was different. The train was thronged with men, young and middle-aged (some, I swear, in anoraks). Though they were scattered through the coaches, sitting alone or in small groups, they seemed to know each other or at least be nodding acquaintances. Now and again they'd rise and roam along the train, exchanging a word or two with the others. Some studied railway books or notebooks closely printed with lists of numbers. They spoke in English accents (the loudest from Bradford) and from eavesdropping I gathered that most had come north on overnight trains.

As we emerged from Cowlairs tunnel and passed through Springburn they pressed noses to the windows and peered out at Eastfield depot, where locomotives were lined up under harsh orange lights waiting for the day's duty. Then the penny dropped. They were loco-spotters. I beg their pardon, I mustn't say that. I was told off for it. Loco-spotters? They were pilgrims. They had gathered to mourn the passing of the diesel in the west.

'We've come to mark the end of diesel-hauled trains on the West Highland line', I was told by the man from Bradford. The following week the familiar throaty rumble of diesels was to be silenced on this route, to be replaced by the insubstantial clatter of Sprinter sets. I was assisting at a wake.

Some of the mourners alighted with me at Tyndrum and we made a beeline for the red light of the Little Chef and breakfast. I climbed my hill, Ben Udlaith (the Dark or Gloomy One). The day was bleak and grey, and a strong wind was blowing thin sheets of rain. Somewhere in the gloom I heard muffled shots and hoped no one would mistake my figure on the skyline for quarry. Stalkers don't do that, do they? Coming down into the dusky valley of the Orchy I had to pick my way through new forest planting, awkward ground trenched by drainage ditches and accursed by walkers.

When the train came in to take me back there were mourners aboard as before. Bradford man was there, having journeyed the long way to Mallaig and back. For some reason he got out at Garelochhead, which is nothing more than a halt above bright lights shining on the water. No doubt he had reason to expect some locomotive stir. I heard others discussing plans for their arrival in Glasgow. One intended to call at Eastfield and then take a taxi across the city to find the second last diesel in a particular class still at work. Then he'd return to the city centre in time to catch the night train to Bristol. This twenty-four hours in that man's life sounded to me like hell on wheels, in slow motion.

All the same, I share his regret for the passing of the diesels. Trains are not the same fun now.

4
Across the map

Corrour on a bad day is like the edge of the known world. Corrour is a platform, a signal box, a house, and a billboard advertising Morgan's Den, a bunkhouse I've not had the pleasure of lodging in, and hope never to. It is 1,300 feet above sea level at the highest point on the West Highland railway from Glasgow to Fort William, where the moorland meets wild hills. There is no road. On the big faded map of Scotland which used to lean against a wall in the newspaper office where I worked it wasn't even dignified as a station. Simply Corrour Siding, a dot on the thin black line that wound across empty country.

That morning Corrour was my starting point on a week's trek across country. I thought I'd climb hills on the way, and at journey's end I'd see Mary. I'd recently met Mary while tramping the West Highland Way and we'd become good walking companions and close friends. The thought of being with her spurred me on and put a spring in my step.

I emerged from a warm train into a hostile environment. No one was about. I stood alone on the platform as the train slid away to merge with the landscape. The hills were freshly slabbed with snow. A sudden cold snap had broken a long spell of spring sunshine and after a sharp overnight frost it was bitterly cold.

Thin ice glazed the black bog pools as I set out on the turf path alongside the railway line, and a chill wind from the north tugged at my woolly hat and gloves. Above me on the embankment a train of wagons rumbled past. There was a hoot from the locomotive and I caught sight of an arm waving from the cab.

As I descended beside a burn that tumbled over platforms of rock I could see distant Loch Treig silvered by sunshine, and on the way to it I met two walkers, a man and a woman, unbelievably in shirt sleeves. 'Aren't you cold?' said I, aghast. 'No', they replied blithely, 'we've been sunbathing by the loch'. Apparently they'd found a rocky suntrap on the shore. I could hardly credit it, and by the time I reached the loch all trace of sun had disappeared and mist was drifting over the white bulk of Stob Coire Easain on the far shore.

Beyond the head of the loch the path led steeply through a rocky defile, after which the cone of Stob Ban came into view, free of the ragged clouds that hovered around the greater hills. Stob Ban, the White Peak – one of several hills with that name – is described in The Munros (the Scottish Mountaineering Club's guidebook to walking the high hills of Scotland) as 'a remote peak, far distant and invisible from any main road'. Since it's not particularly high or testing it offered a reasonable challenge for the afternoon. I left the path to plod upwards through gorse and heather, eventually reaching the snowline. By the time I was nearing the top the rucksack, laden as it was with tent, stove and food for a week, had become an intolerable burden. Why lug it all the way to the top? I swung it off my sweaty back and wedged it upright between two large stones.

The snow that had been mere flecks in the wind began to fall thick and fast and suddenly, to my surprise, I had company in the storm. As I struggled up the last rocky feet a ghostly figure arose over the summit and came striding towards me through the flying snowflakes. A Munroist – well met on the mountain top! He was heading for a bothy, a stone but-and-ben just visible on flat ground at the foot of the mountain, where he and two companions were holed up for the week. As I watched him lope off downhill I came to an instant decision; the prospect of a night under canvas in such weather was not enticing and if a bothy was there it ought to be slept in.

I paused at the top only to take a photo of my ice axe embedded in the cairn with its strap flying madly in the wind, then hurried down to retrieve my pack. At first I couldn't find it. Panic. The new snow had blotted out all minor lumps and bumps with a thin, uniform blanket, and to add to the confusion the slope was littered higgledy-piggledy with rocks and stones, among which my rucksack was perfectly camouflaged. The lesson is this: sticky-out bits seen from below will merge seamlessly with the landscape when looked down upon from above. This is an absolute rule. I searched and searched, and then almost stumbled on the pack by chance, all blotched with white.

Here the Munro book recommends a detour: 'The return can be pleasantly varied by descending over boulder scree to the bealach [Gaelic for saddle]. From there go down a giant's staircase of quartzite slabs . . . ' Pleasantly varied be damned. My one ambition was to get to the bottom of the hill and into the bothy fast, avoiding if possible anything remotely like a staircase, especially the giant kind.

By the time I reached level ground it was blowing a helter-skelter blizzard. I squelched across the burn, kicked the snow off my boots on the threshold and lifted the latch. Inside was good cheer. A fire was flickering up the lum thanks to the efforts of the ghost from the summit, whom I found established and clashing the cooking pots. The bothy was bare, stone-walled and furnished only with an old sagging sofa and a white plastic cooking shelf mottled by ingrained food stains and cigarette burns. On this greasy worktop was piled an accumulation of stove, cups, plates (dirty), open milk carton and food packets, among which the stranger was preparing a dish of spaghetti.

My meal was duller. I carried all my meals on my back, intending to cook them in a tent. All were freeze-dried. Mostly they had exotic titles and tonight I selected creole turkey. Pour boiling water in the packet, stir, rest for five minutes, stir again and eat. Mmmm.

I wouldn't say it was unpleasant. It was spicy, I'll give it that. Chunks of white meat were recognisable in the glutinous sauce, small and tough to be sure, but edible. For a turn, creole turkey would do. I didn't know it then, but creole turkey was to be the best of it. In a week of degenerating dining, the thought of good honest plain food increasingly became a tantalising dream.

There came a clumping at the door and in burst two tired climbers, mates of the cook, shaking the snow off their backs like shaggy dogs. They'd had a bad experience. In the course of a circuit of peaks one had become exhausted and sat down in the snow – 'just to take a rest'. His friend had to force him on; otherwise, who knows? Shut-eye in a snowstorm could be your last.

They shed their soaking outer garments, lodged themselves elbow to elbow in the distressed sofa and forked up spaghetti hungrily, their faces ruddy in the firelight glow. I sat on a large stone on the hearth with a mug of coffee steaming in my hands and my right buttock gently toasting. Later a whisky bottle was brought out for a nightcap and handed round from one to the other. Seated on my warm stone, I prepared to accept a glass, but it wasn't offered. Hospitality didn't stretch to strangers. So dramless to bed, on bare planks in the loft.

Dawn broke crisp and clear with the land all white. The snowfall had laid some inches on the bare earth and everywhere glinted in the sun. I debated which way to turn. To the left was Sgurr Innse, a rocky pudding basin of a hill, 'a dramatic wee peak', in the words of Hamish Brown. Though it looked like a good scramble I turned my back on it in favour of Stob Coire Easain, a higher but less adventurous peak, a hodden grey sort of hill. Even to get near it involved a trauchle through deep snow, only to find the higher slopes dispiritingly steep, especially when I was burdened by the dead weight of a laden rucksack. I was tempted to ditch it again but thought better of it in view of the previous day's alarm. Some few hundred feet from the top, on a stiff ascent and a treacherous surface, I came to a halt and decided that life was not designed to be such slow torture. I aborted the climb.

It retrospect I did myself no favour. Instead of a fancy-free ridgewalk along the crest I was faced with an awkward sidelong tramp along the contours of a rough hillside. Though the summits had misted over and I'd have seen nothing from the tops, the walking would have been pleasanter. I was forever plunging in and out of snow-filled gullies, and during my slow progress towards the valley of the Spean and my goal, the village of Fersit, I was constantly buffeted by squalls. I could see them wheeling over distant glens and racing towards me, spitting needle-sharp pellets, and later, as the temperature rose a little, whiskering my face with soft wet flakes.

On the tail of the ridge at last I could look down on the black headwaters of Loch Treig and the railway line that runs parallel with its shore, a continuation of the West Highland line I'd left the day before. I considered pitching my tent but no obvious camp site appeared. Here the ground was too rough, there it was stony or too exposed. Not that I worried; I knew of a private hostel at Fersit and the thought of another night under cover of a roof was seductive.

A fingerpost pointed into woodland where the hostel was revealed to be a couple of caravans and a ramshackle timber cottage. I walked up a path lined with daffodils and was about to try the door when a small white-haired woman in a woolly jumper and cord trousers came round the corner: this was Nancy Smith, the perky chatelaine (now dead, alas). Nancy led me into the tiny living room and put a match to the black stove which burst into flaming life with a satisfactory roar. A pot big enough to boil a small missionary in sat on the stove – the only source of hot water on the premises. In fact, because of some hiatus in the system there was no running water at all. It had to be fetched from a tap outside, and the loo was a hutch round the back with a chemical bucket and a heap of bracken and heather beside it to hide the evidence. Beside the stove was a battered writing desk and on the wainscotted walls were shelves stuffed with old Scots Magazines and National Geographics. A few curling posters advertised long-past folk concerts by such as the Corries. A galley kitchen opened off the room, stocked with pots and pans and jazzy with colour photos and postcards from former guests.

I liked it. Now and again Nancy looked in from her own quarters next door.

36

'Make yourself at home', she said – and I did. Nancy's hostel was cosy. And best of all I had it to myself.

After a meal I sat by the stove reading and writing before going to bed in a cubicle of a dormitory. Above my bed was a faded colour print of a Tyrolean peasant girl outside her cottage under the Matterhorn. The floor had a visible tilt and the top bunk on which I lay had a similar rake. Sleep was a sloping experience.

Snow fell lightly in the night. When I woke and looked through the little window framed with blue check curtains I saw daffodils drooping in the cold and bare birch trees dotted with white. That morning I left the big rucksack behind and, with a light day sack, did the rounds of a couple of Munros, Stob Coire Sgriodain and Chno Dearg, with the lesser Meall Garbh thrown in. Ptarmigan were about in the rocky tops, camouflaged in winter plumage of white and grey. Later in the day I came upon big herds of deer in the glens, equally well camouflaged on the russet lower slopes. Once I found a deer carcase at my feet, one of several I saw in the next few days. It had been a bad winter for deer. All over Scotland they died from cold and wet and lack of feeding – and from the fact that there were just too many of them to thrive. Now opinion has moved in favour of culling rather than encouraging numbers, which is a good thing for all concerned – for the forester, the naturalist, the keeper and even the so-called sportsman. The deer themselves will fare better, or at least those that escape the bullet.

After two nights at Nancy's I left with regret. But by now I was thinking of my rendezvous. I had ground to cover and little time to climb any more hills. The morning was mild and for the first time I set out bare-headed and without gloves. Birds sang in the airless forest.

Over high open moorland I followed a track that took me across a broken plank bridge, all askew, down to Strathossian House (Ossian slept here?), a lodge sheltered in a clump of trees. Fresh horse droppings lay in the courtyard in front of the stables, so someone had been about recently, though I saw no one. The lodge stands at the meeting of passes, and conscious of the miles to be covered I took the low road, finding a barely visible track along the shores of a dark loch. Now the weather menaced again and big fleecy snowflakes filled the sky. Crossing a tumbling burn was no easy matter. I trudged back and forth along the bank before finding a spot where I could trust myself to a hop and a jump over the boulder-filled torrent.

The track led me to open ground where a ruin marked on the map as Lubvan stood in a patch of level sward, the perfect camp site. But I felt it was too early to halt. Once again the clouds lowered and a steady rain began to fall. All day I'd been alone in the landscape. I'd not seen a soul since waving goodbye to Nancy; the day had been mine. But no longer. The spell was broken by a distant figure on a bicycle with a pack on his back, pedalling briskly across my line of sight through the curtain of rain. Where had he been? Where was he going? Questions never to be answered for our paths didn't join. He wheeled off in the direction of Loch Laggan and the road through Glen Spean. I decided to camp on a small hillside and while looking for a site another walker tramped by. He was lost and looking for the companion he'd parted from in the mist. Our brief exchange was the only conversation I had all day.

It was spotting with rain when I crawled into the tent for my first night in the open. The tent was a thin green tube and the roof bulged down to within inches of my chest, and I felt like Jonah in the belly of the whale. I drifted to sleep lullabied by raindrops pattering lightly overhead.

I woke in the night and touched the tent roof, and it was wet. Must be leaking. Damned tent! On rising in the morning I discovered otherwise. When I unzipped the flap and struggled out the whole tent tinkled. An icicle hung at the bell end and the outer skin was coated in frost. The wet inside must have been condensation – no wonder I'd shivered in the night.

But no regrets. I was looking at clear skies. The white hills were flushed shell pink in the dawn and there was birdsong. Blue sky, crisp air, light clouds drifting from mountain tops. Prominent among the hills were the corrie-riven Beinn a'Chlachair and the mighty Aonach Beag, both unassailable, alas, in my new scheme of things. I had to press on.

With the sun on my face I crossed a sturdy timber bridge over a wide, deep stream with a sandy bottom glinting below. Nearby was the handsome pile of Binnein Shuas which had been a marker for me the day before, and ahead was rugged Creag Pitridh, beloved by rock climbers. I rounded Pitridh's southern spur and climbed beside a burn into the pass between Beinn a'Clachair and Geal Charn, big hills both, snowy mountains spread out on either hand like angels' wings. In the deep snow at the top I lost the path, and momentarily my way. Following my nose rather than the compass I stopped short on the brink of a steep drop into the deep-set Loch a' Bhealaich Leambain, a grey pool filling a narrow corrie far below. How best to negotiate these treacherous slopes? The ground fell sharply, the true nature of the slope masked by a white pavement of cornice. Then I took stock and realised that a descent to the lochan would take me the wrong way entirely. I turned back thankfully, and none too soon, for there was a sudden rushing sound like an express train. I could see nothing but it must have been a cornice collapsing somewhere in the neighbourhood, and I was pleased then that I hadn't ventured into the gully. I climbed to another watershed and slithered into Coire a'Mhaigh, plunging into soft snow where the course of a burn was marked only by a line of pot-holes between high snowy banks.

By this time, five days out, the exertion was beginning to tell on me. My back hurt. My pack felt like lead, and hoisting it on to my shoulders became an increasing challenge. I developed a technique to give my shoulders a rest, bending double to make a table of my back. Thus I saw many a landscape through my legs, upside down. It gives mountain scenery a fresh perspective.

Once on firmer ground I slumped on to a smooth rock beside the burn, eased the rucksack off and spoke into a mini recorder – my way of keeping a diary en route. The tape relays a small plaintive voice saying, 'I'm sitting by a waterfall with my head in my hands, on a rock, exhausted'.

There were still miles to go. I came down through woodland towards Loch Laggan and a miniature Balmoral, the granite house of Ardverikie, grey, turreted and Scots baronial. Piles of felled timber made abstract sculpture along the verges of the tarred estate road that runs the length of the loch. A few cars and Land-Rovers passed and I got the occasional nod. At the head of the loch I crossed the River Pattack and walked briefly on the A86 Fort William to Kingussie, the first public road I'd set foot on since leaving Glasgow. Then I turned on to open heath, where I'd have camped but for lack of water. Hard as I looked, not the merest trickle could I find among the heather slopes. I descended into Glen Shirra where the young Spey bulges out into a man-made loch, dammed by the hydro board. The sky was sunless and heavily overcast and a chill wind had risen.

I pitched camp as best I could in tussocky grass and prepared a last evening meal, following the usual pattern. Packet soup with a stock cube and lump of butter added, followed by freeze-dried main course, and then stewed prunes for pudding. Dull, dull. Soup was warm and nourishing, prunes were healthy, but how I came to hate the freeze-dry packs that came between! Exotic by name and nasty by nature. Breakfasts were better, except that the daily muesli now tasted like sawdust. The cheese had mouldered. The one true soother and reviver proved to be a mug of cocoa last thing at night, best with a dash of brandy or rum in it. Drink that and snug in your tent you're back in the womb.

Rat-a-tat-tat went the woodpecker in the trees. Time to get up. I rose and made ready. Packing had become a small ordeal, taking longer day by day. My fingers had become tender due to the cold and the constant pushing, pulling, pinching, squeezing and snapping of straps, laces, belts and buckles. They became so sensitive that it was difficult even to snap open the plastic food bags.

Gulls and peewits congregated at the dam and rose in chattering drifts. The Monadhliath Mountains loomed dark, bleak and snowy, and I hurried along General Wade's road by the marshy margin of the loch. After passing the lochside house of Sherrabeg I came upon the Badenoch anglers' shack with a notice nailed to it saying Lunch Hut. I had a vision here. I saw a plump, shiny-faced lady in a full-sailed pinny dispensing mugs of hot broth and sensible food like mince, tatties, carrot and turnip. I guess the truth is more mundane. More likely wet anglers shelter here to munch wodgy sandwiches from plastic boxes. The buxom matron of the lunch hut was the figment of a fevered mind.

Beyond the head of the loch the road rose. Parked on a knoll in a neighbouring field stood a caravan from which issued, on my approach, a troop of barking dogs of several varieties, tumbling out in an excited state; terriers, retrievers and large, lolloping flap-eared hounds of no breed I recognised, pell-mell. All bayed at me from behind the fence. A tousled, grey-haired woman followed them, vainly trying to bring them to heel. She was like the old woman who lived in a shoe – so many dogs she didn't know what to do.

The nascent River Spey winds through a wide, flat valley in meadows crowded with sheep. From here I made the last ascent of the trek, up a grassy brae to Blairgie Crag and then eastwards along a ridge of wet moorland, with views across the glen and, in the distance, towards my destination, the village of Newtonmore on the road to Aviemore and Inverness. Finally I dropped down through steep rocky bluffs into the heathery valley of the River Calder, where tributaries which looked formidably wide on the map turned out to be shallow, stony-bedded and easily forded.

When I reached the outskirts of Newtonmore the Saturday strollers gazed blankly as I trudged past with a whole week weighing down on my shoulders. Here at last was the small hotel where Mary and I had stayed once before, and here were hosts Andy and Erica at the door to greet me. But where was Mary, the one I longed to see? Not there. A message had come instead. A son was ill and she couldn't leave him. So at night I dined on my own and went to bed alone, and for lack of my love's soft embrace sank gently into the arms of Morpheus.

5

New boots in Knoydart

Chris Brasher sat on a log at the edge of the sea and took off his
boots. 'Try these', he said, handing them to me, still warm from his
feet – a perfect fit. I still have them. Until recently I wore them for
light walking, though by then they'd aged, got scuffed and down at
heel and threatened to disintegrate (which sounds like me).

Chris Brasher, Olympic gold medallist turned conservationist,
was a big man in boots. His company manufactured them, and with
other outdoors writers I'd been invited to Knoydart to try out the
gear. Knoydart is a wild peninsula, one of those desolate areas on
the north-west coast of Scotland aptly known as the Rough
Bounds. There's no easy way in. To get there you face a long walk
or you come by sea.

The hot sun of May beat down on the fishing port of Mallaig
and holidaymakers wore shirt sleeves and summer frocks. Waiting
for Alan Robinson's boat, three of us sat on a bollard and licked ice
cream, watched the black and white herring boats, the black and
white seagulls, and the pink-skinned people.

Alan Robinson is a short, greybearded Englishman who used
to build boats in Cornwall. As trade declined he looked for
something else, and while sailing off the west coast of Scotland he
caught sight of a tumbledown cottage on Doune Bay in Knoydart.
He bought the ruin and converted it with his own hands and the
help of his sons Toby and Jamie. They built a lodge, an up-market
bunkhouse close by, and from this base he operates a business taking
parties on fishing, boating and nature expeditions.

The Mary Doune, launched not long before and named after
his wife and his home, was his second motor cruiser. Once aboard
we made a straight wake over blue water rimmed by a coastline of
astounding beauty – a Hebridean idyll, at least while the weather
lasted. Disembarking at a high wooden quay, we joined the rest of

the party, which included Cameron McNeish, climber, editor of an outdoors magazine and future presenter of TV programmes on wilderness walks; the writer and ecologist Jim Crumley; backpacker and writer Chris Townsend; also Alan Thomson, a photo-journalist and former newspaper colleague of mine. And there was Rob, a tubby, affable man who managed all weekend to avoid setting foot on any hill. Rob was there to promote his products, made in a factory in Blairgowrie, including an environmentally friendly foot spray (no aerosol) and an insecticide called Bug Off. Bug Off helped to slay many midges, and I'm grateful to the man for that, but there was to be an occasion when I'd gladly have bugged off big Rob.

That night we had a delayed launching party for the Mary Doune. Local friends had been invited and could be seen approaching from afar, cresting a nearby hill like Indians in a Western. Knoydart is thinly populated and neighbours have to tramp from miles away. Two rode up on mountain bikes and some were camping on the machair. On trenchers in the kitchen were platters of seafood caught that day. Friends, neighbours, climbers, walkers and boot people wandered round the kitchen picking at titbits, filling glasses, or sat themselves at the big plank table outside. Then the liberty dinghy took us by boatloads to where the Mary Doune floated at her mooring. Champagne flowed and the sun set over a calm sea to a hubbub of sociable chatter.

Sunshine had spoilt us and next morning we wore shorts in expectation of another scorcher. Offshore, waiting for us, the Mary Doune sat mirrored in still waters, only pale fingers of thin cloud in the sky above. With land and sea still glazed in delicate early sunshine we sheared crystal water on our way round Knoydart's north coast into Loch Hourn and a landfall on a seaweedy strand in Barisdale Bay.

A welcoming party waited on the shingle, led by Paul Jarvis, professor of forestry and natural resources at Edinburgh University. He and his team were busy putting back the ecological clock. Working on behalf of the John Muir Trust they aimed to renew the old Scots pine woodland that had once covered much of these parts before sheep and too many deer turned it into a green desert. Jarvis and helpers gathered seed from the remaining Barisdale pines, had them grown on in nurseries, and in due course planted out the seedlings. Another John Muir party was busy up the glen ditching and draining to preserve the track that zigzags up from Barisdale into Coire Dhorrcail; a necessary task, for the wildnerness character of Knoydart – still inaccessible by road – is being eroded as increasing numbers of walkers breach its rugged frontiers. Remote Knoydart is getting busier by the year.

Ladhar Bheinn is 'a mountain of soaring ridges, spectacular corries, testing remoteness and stunning panoramic views'; I quote from Ralph Storer's book 100 Best Routes on Scottish Mountains. Storer calls it the most beautiful mountain in the British Isles, but for me beauty implies a grace which the muscular Ladhar Bheinn lacks, whatever else its appeal.

Black crags above us were disappearing into puffs of white mist as we left the tree planters and started to climb. Brasher, in a gaudy environmentally unfriendly scarlet cap, had notions of diverting to find the track-building party but was silently outvoted. There was a challenging hill ahead and we were wearing his boots – what more did the man want? Once we'd topped the skyline at the head of Coire Dhorrcail we were rewarded by an exciting scramble along a narrow ridge, notionally offering dazzling views over successive waves of hills and long reaches of water, but blanked out on that day by a dull haze. A sudden chill breeze raised goosepimples on bare thighs and trousers were pulled on.

There is a distinct curvature in the long spine of Ladhar Bheinn. It kinks this way and that, directing the walker to all points of the compass in the course of a long traverse. We veered south-eastwards on to another steeply dropping ridge, well trodden only recently, judging by the broken cover of soft soil crumbling away from the bedrock. The way led along the edge of cliffs falling plumb into the corrie, and I can picture yet the figure of Paddy, one of the boot people and a veteran hill runner, admiring the view from the lip of a sheer drop. Lean and stringy and in his sixties, with a white frisking beard round his leprechaun face, he stood like an emaciated figurehead on a rocky prow.

Muriel Gray sailed down from these heights clutched in the arms of a paraglider as a climax to her TV Munro Show, but we had to foot it all the way. Two parties in turn peeled off at different stages of the ridgewalk to head for lower ground and the Land-Rover waiting to pick us up in the glen, but three of us – Paddy, Chris Townsend and I – kept to the high ground to the bitter end, a grey sting in the tail called Sgurr Coire Choinnichean. Paddy and Chris spent a lot of time discussing mountain marathons, which appeal to them but not to me. It's Paddy's nature to break into a run whenever the terrain offers the faintest excuse, and so it was then. The Sgurr escarpment slope was clad in close-cropped, springy turf and this was a carrot to Paddy's donkey. He broke into a brisk trot, Chris followed and I, perforce, lumbered in pursuit. It was a fast descent – something like 2,500 feet in half an hour.

The beer at the seafront pub in Inverie goes down even faster. But it was only a refreshing interlude. Three mountain bikes had been left for us in a glen by friends who'd climbed Ladhar Bheinn in the reverse direction. The bikes, which had to be taken back to Doune, had been duly retrieved by our party and ridden in relays to Inverie, the half-way stage. Some preordained logic which I did not fully understand now dictated that those who were last off the mountain (and who had thus made the greatest physical effort), namely Chris, Paddy and I, should pedal the last lap while the rest took a lift in the Land-Rover.

Nonstop Paddy didn't even pause for a drink. No sooner had we arrived than he was in the saddle and whizzing off at a fast clip. Sometime later Chris and I strolled out to make our choice of the two remaining bikes (I got the pink one) and I mounted painfully. It was the first time in many years that I'd ridden a bicycle, and my first time ever on a mountain bike. Chris soon outpaced me. Wrestling with a bewildering variety of gears, I was grounded while attempting a steep slope in the wrong combination. There was no drama, no header over the handlebars, I just shuddered to a halt and tumbled over in slow motion. At this point the Land-Rover passed, full of cheering (jeering?) faces.

Six miles to go. I decided that since there was no call for speed I might as well enjoy the spin. After all, the sky had cleared and the evening had turned fine. Where the path to Doune joined the road I left my bike with the two others already propped against a signpost, and stretched out gratefully on the springy turf. The descending sun glowed warmly, the sea glittered, the blue island of Eigg spread languorously across the horizon, birds sang. I savoured peace and contentment for a while before strolling back over the sweet-scented moorland to the lodge and a welcome shower.

That night we all dined in the cottage, seated round the big table that Alan Robinson had fashioned from a solid balk of dark timber from his former boatyard. We sat crowded in the little dining room with its drawings of yachts on the wall and seafaring bric-a-brac on the mantelshelf, watching the sky grow fiery red over the peaked mountains of Skye. Then Cameron and Jim took their guitars and dinner drifted into ceilidh time. I was wise enough to leave at a respectable hour, picking my way across the rocky causeway that led to the lodge, with the stars shining and the sounds of folksong lingering in the air.

Now a veil should be drawn. This is when the balm of sleep should have soothed the pain of a hard day, but no. On this night big Rob, who slept opposite Chris Brasher and me, proved himself a virtuoso trumpeter. His snores have a wealth of baroque ornamentation and the repertoire is played for the most part fortissimo. At intervals throughout the night there was an audible impatient tossing of bodies in adjacent bunks, and as the skies began to lighten blurred figures could be seen stirring uneasily. Chris Brasher was moved to hurl a foot spray at its unconscious maker, but without effect. I contemplated severer methods. The Boot, perhaps? I imagined a pattern of corrugations matching the Brasher sole imprinted on the flesh of the snorer. At least the night was illumined by a vision. She swam into view in the half-light before dawn, a pale female figure which in my fevered state of mind seemed to be naked. She hovered silently over the sleeping trumpeter. I peeped over the blanket and then averted my eyes. It could not be real.

Breakfast at the big table and promise of a fine morning restored our spirits (Rob, of course, felt fine). This time the Mary Doune turned southwards, rounding a rocky foreland into Loch Nevis, a loch that is almost cut in two by a sandy neck of land, beyond which it opens into a small lagoon like a condom end. The morning was breathless and the water glassy as we cut speed and crawled through the narrows. On either side were spits of land on which two or three white cottages (one of which, a fortnight later, was burned to a blackened shell in a disastrous and fatal fire). Ahead, the tapering blue-rinse peak of Sgurr na Ciche was mirrored pencil-sharp in the still water. It was fairyland. Then the Mary Doune broke the peace, churned water abruptly, and brought us into Camusrory, where a high concrete pier provided the first challenge of the day: how to scale the long vertical ladder with a pack on your back.

After a bit we left the path and climbed straight up the hillside. The leaders set a relentless pace. Early midges were out – but not to worry, we had protection. I dashed the snorer's nostrum on my face and arms, and it worked. The drawback was that as I grew hotter the sweat and the Bug Off seemed to react together on my skin, and finally I washed it all off again in a burn.

The top of Meall Buidhe, or yellow hill (which it isn't) provided a welcome respite, but it was decided that with one Munro under our belts we ought to polish off the neighbouring Luinne Bheinn, a mountain equally barren, more or less the same height and just as steep. The distance between them is almost two miles as the crow flies and the crow has the best of it. Walkers have to alter course according to the lie of the land. This meant descending into the Bealach Ile Coire, and then over a lumpy stretch where lochans lie in the flatlands of Coire Odhair. There was now an unpleasant breeze blowing and a hint of mist when we reached the summit ridge and made for the small cairn. Luinne Bheinn (Loony Bin according to jokers) translates variously as the angry hill, the happy hill or the singing hill, according to choice, but on that day it was a sullen hill. The view was disappointing and we didn't stay long.

It was a long haul to Inverie where we were to meet the Mary Doune and her master. We set off down the rock-strewn hillside and on lower grassy slopes Paddy broke into his usual run, soon joined by Cameron, and their figures diminished in the distance. It was a weary way; long miles, mostly on the hard surface of a tractor track, until at last we reached a lane shaded by old rhododendrons in the policies of Inverie House.

It was the Sabbath. The pub was shut and we could only linger on the pier waiting for the Mary Doune to arrive and take us over to Mallaig. The pubs were shut there too. Mallaig on a Sunday out of season is a very presbyterian place.

Later I did my bit for the forest in Knoydart. Having been impressed by the work of Paul Jarvis and his team, I joined the John Muir Trust and signed on for a tree-planting weekend.

The John Muir Trust is named after a Scots emigrant who became the apostle of the American wilderness. His book My First Summer in the Sierra, describing a journey into the Sierra Nevada mountains of California, is one of my favourites. The trust was founded in the eighties by Chris Brasher and others with the aim of acquiring and maintaining wild land in its unspoilt condition, subject to the needs of people living there. One of its first actions was to buy part of Knoydart when the Ministry of Defence sought to acquire it for war games.

Shreds of the Old Caledonian Forest can still be found, if you're fit enough, in its remote glens. Once when Prince Charles visited, he helicoptered in, but we had to walk. Though there's a good track all the way from the road-end at the village of Kinloch Hourn, it's a rugged tramp all of six miles. In compensation there's a prospect of wonderful mountain scenery.

Four of us tree planters walked in as the setting sun lit up the sky behind Ladhar Bheinn's snowy southern cone. The rays illuminated a great pine tree that had been laid low in a recent gale, now measuring its length on a rocky outcrop above Loch Hourn, its foliage still green. We made slow progress because one of us – not a seasoned walker – had blistered her feet badly and had to hobble. Darkness fell before we arrived and the last couple of miles were covered by the light of head torches. We saw no one until we passed the bothy at Barisdale, not far from our destination. Through the window we glimpsed ruddy faces lit by a flickering fire and there was fiddle music. By the look of the bottles and cans on the table the ceilidh had been going with a swing for some time.

Planting seedling pine trees amid the rugged scenery of the west Highlands may seem a pleasant way of passing a weekend but there was a considerable drawback. It was March and the weather was changeable. The bright beckoning sunshine of the past few days had gone with a vengeance, to be succeeded by leaden skies. A keen wind blew and a drenching rain fell throughout the day. As dawn struggled into meagre daylight it seemed nicer to stay in bed, except that bed was a sleeping bag on the bare floor of an abandoned cottage, grandly known as the White House, a damp and chilly place and on this occasion grossly overcrowded. Nineteen people jostled in its tiny rooms. I found a bed space in an upstairs room with half the panelling ripped off the walls and ceiling, and a hole in the bare boards of the floor. Even wearing thermal vest and long johns, I shivered in my sleeping bag. Since the cottage had been offered by the landowner I shouldn't grumble. It was better than a tent.

Our work-site was a knob of ground overlooking the Dhorrcail burn as it gushes through a gorge on its way to debouch into Loch Hourn. To get there involved crossing a stretch of marshland and gaining six hundred feet of height by a stalker's path. A mile, they said it would be, but this, take note, was a Highland mile and Highland miles for sure are longer. When I arrived, late, John Muirites hooded in cagoules were dotted all over the soggy hillside with spades and buckets and it looked like a mad seaside outing. I was given a spade, a bag of young pines and a quick course of instruction. You pick a likely spot (a rough guide: heather is fine for pine, bracken OK for oak), scrape off as much vegetation as you can with a few slices of the spade, and then cut out roughly a square foot of turf. You ease the spade under the turf, prize it up and give it a twist so that it flops upside down – but not back in the hole from which you've dug it, which swiftly floods with rain and ground water. You make an incision in the upturned turf, place a green shoot in it and bed it down with a few stamps of the boot. You've planted a pine tree.

Infant pines are some six inches in length with a whorl of shoots at the top covered in a fuzz of soft green needles. It's hard to picture them in maturity, fifty or sixty feet tall and maybe more, with a deep-etched crust of bark and a spreading crown of lustrous dark green carried on twisting boughs. And yet not so hard, for two or three miles away the aged parents of these seedlings are found growing tall in the glen, spreading from the hillside down to the banks of the Barisdale river. In life is death. Here and there are gaunt reminders of mortality; dead trunks standing stripped of their bark, gale-wrecked giants stretched lifeless on the earth surrounded by their writhing root and branch systems.

We walked back to the cottage by way of the coast, high above the loch, where a small boat bobbed in shallow water over shelving sand, beside a bright red buoy. The sea was a delicate ultramarine shading into deep purple, barred with darker strands where beds of seaweed grew. Even on this dreich day it gleamed like a tropical lagoon.

6

The Aga can't

Jet planes training for future wars thundered through the glens near
the Commando monument at Spean Bridge, where a green patina
has aged the three bronze figures in battledress. I parked among
trees between lochs Lochy and Arkaig and followed a forest walk
through sunlit glades. Tall trees masked the river in its gorge, or
parted to give glimpses of green hillsides. Two miles on I reached
the open hill at the head of the glen. Below conic Meall an
Tagraidh lay the ruined house of Fedden with bare, roofless,
tumbledown walls and a gaunt chimney stack poking up in the
middle.

A platter of bogland separates the slopes of Meall an Tagraidh
and the greater Sron a'Choire Ghairbh (the Neb of the Rugged
Corrie). The neb's southwest shoulder is circumvented by a path –
fainter on the ground than on the map – leading to a col, from
where a zigzag track assaults the final steep slope. This stalker's track
is a masterpiece of the art, a canny feat of route-making which eases
the gradient and gives a sound base for the boot. It leads almost to
the top, where a pop-up picture book of views unfolds, a reward
after being so long hemmed in by forest and glen. Long Loch
Lochy and its satellite, pinched Loch Oich, linked by a thread of
Caledonian Canal, extended far along the Great Glen. Bulky Ben
Nevis and its attendants, veined in snow, filled the southern space,
and westwards spread the jagged skyline of the Morar and Lochaber
hills.

Hastening down the zigzags, I met a walker coming up. He
was making dour progress and prepared to pause only briefly in
passing. He was on his last day out and had to be back in
Edinburgh that evening. From the pass below I worked round an
eminence called Meall Dubh to reach the steep grassy slopes of
Meall na Teanga (Tongue Hill), my second Munro of the day,

though it only just scrapes by at a height of 3,012 feet.

My route continued along a short stretch of skyline ridge with a lump of rock on it to be scrambled over. Steep slopes fell on one side to Loch Lochy and on the other to the flat-bottomed corridor between the hills where Lochan Fhudair and many small waters sparkled. A tiny pleasure boat cut a white way through the fierce blue of Lochy, and faint wah-wahs from its tannoy commentary came wafting upwards. We were in two elements, I in the sky and they on water. Were binoculars raised in my direction from the deck? I was vain enough to think so, so I put on the style just in case, making a spurt for a bit.

The long walk back through the trees was hot and sticky, and I shed my shirt to shower in the waterfall that spouted over rocks at the forestry car park. I'd have stripped off altogether if picknickers hadn't been about.

I found a B&B beside Loch Lochy. The black labrador of the house was at his dinner on the edge of the drive and too busy to take notice when I drove up; his snout remained fixed in the dish, and so did mine later, metaphorically, when I dined off a linen cloth among guests – tourists all and not a walker among them – whose conversations were tuned to a genteel murmur. The loudest noise was the clatter of cutlery. Next morning my landlady provided the best sandwiches I've yet tasted on the hill, rough bread buttered with beef and a leaf of lettuce and just enough mayonnaise to moisten but not squelch. I took my first bite while huddling in a drystane shelter near the top of Gleouraich (the Groaner) on the north side of Loch Quoich.

Gone was the sunshine of the day before, although it was muggy by the loch side and the midges were biting. But the glinting light had turned to a leaden grey, the loch waters were lacklustre, and for good measure the dam and its kindred buildings were the ugliest of their kind. A line of pylons tramped over the hillside where a few dead trees stripped to the bare pole did nothing to enliven the scene. Not a hilltop was visible in the blanket mist.

But pink and red rhododendrons gave cheer to the roadside as I searched among them for the path. 'A cairn on the west side of the stream marks the rhododendron-overgrown start', states the Munro book, but where was the cairn? I saw the bridge, the burn, the trees, the bushes. I knew where I was and I found the path, such as it was, but I'm blessed if I saw the cairn. That rickle of stones in the undergrowth? – surely not. Some purists I know kick down any cairns they find and maybe it had happened here. I discovered what one author (Ralph Storer) calls 'the finest mountain path in the Western Highlands', and sure enough it was a pleasure and privilege to walk it. It led steadily upwards for 2,500 feet to the aforementioned drystane shelter or hide where generations of stalkers have no doubt tucked into lunch and a dram. I was glad of this shield against the wind, which blew keenly, laden with a myriad mist-forming droplets. Six hundred feet above was the rocky top of Gleouraich, which I've called the Groaner but other writers, guessing wildly, interpret variously as 'the noisy hill' or 'a place of uproar'. Not a sound that day, only my raised hood flapping in the wind. Since then Gleouraich has spelt gloom to me, remembering clinging mist and a smirr of rain. There's a trig pillar at the top but somehow I missed it. All I remember is a big cairn. I knew I was at the top because there was nowhere higher to go.

I descended by rocky crests and climbed again by a stiff, stony incline to the next Munro, Spidean Mialach, the Peak of the Deer. This intervening ridgewalk marches along the rim of north-facing precipice walls above three corries in a row, all falling into Easter Glen Quoich. Here the mists parted momentarily to reveal a wet corrie floor and blue hills on the horizon. Working my way down through the gloom I was relieved to see below the cloud line the dark outline of Loch Fearna appear below me – as always in these conditions I'd begun to wonder if I'd got it right.

I returned to the small hotel in Invergarry where I'd earlier booked a room. Shock! The bar didn't open till six, so I soaked in a bath instead. When open, the bar was busy. There was a party of Dutch, and two Englishmen, father and son out of the one mould, both large and lumpish and wearing identical thick spectacles through which they goggled at each other. Father emptied a packet of nuts into one hand, big as a plate, and wolfed them in two gulps. When he sat down to his meal he tucked his tie into his ample waistband and then tucked in.

I had a little attic room with a dormer window which looked over the hotel sign to trees across the road. There was no easy chair, which I'd have liked – there was television and a telephone, neither of which I wanted. When Saturday morning brought sunshine and blue skies again I began to appreciate my little rooftop room. I could hear the rushing river beneath the trees, and rhododendrons were ablaze on the opposite hillside. It looked promising.

I planned to spend the next few days in Glen Shiel climbing the Kintail hills, and so I booked into the Cluanie Inn at the head of Loch Cluanie. This is an old coaching inn and there were brown photos of the way it used to look in early motoring days, a small unostentatious building like a farmhouse with a thin strip of road in front of it and men in bunnets standing at the door. You can see the same sepia scenes in any number of Highland hotels. Since then the place had been extended and spruced up, and more building was about to start which would add chalets and double the amount of accommodation – and possibly the tariff, too.

It was hotter than ever and I changed into shorts before starting the ascent of Aonach Meadhoin, a big hill overlooking the inn on the north side of the glen. It was toilsome but I congratulated myself on being brisk, reaching a cairn (which I took to be the top) in a smart time. I pressed on to the next peak where two heads appeared out of nowhere on the far side of a rubbly ridge. Bodies and legs followed, making the whole man and woman. Talking to them I discovered I'd been careless in reading the map and too smug about my speed. The peak on which I stood was the real Aonach Meadhoin and the earlier one merely its subsidiary, Sgurr an Fhuarail. Never was a name (the Cold Peak) less deserved, for even at 3,000 feet it was sweltering.

I'd also lost the map. Having no deep pocket in my shorts I'd stuck the map in my belt. Somewhere along the way it had fallen out, or else I'd laid it down on a rock and left it. It didn't matter particularly for the weather was settled and I could see where to go, but I felt uneasy about spending the next day or two without a map in an uncertain climate among hills I didn't know.

The couple were en route to their fourth Munro of the day, but I decided to rest content with three. I continued to Sgurr a'Bhealaich Dheirg, the Peak of the Red Pass, whose tower-like cairn sits out all to one side on a promontory of rock slabs. I duly scrambled over to reach it, then followed a narrowing ridge to my final Munro, Saileag, or the Heel, on whose tufted slope I sat down and admired the Five Sisters, the famous five peaks (in fact there are six), the pride of Kintail, and scanned the long stretch of the South Cluanie Ridge on the other side. There I met two hearty veterans, a man and wife who must have been well into their seventies. This pair had taken to the hills only in the past five years or so and were now dashing around making up for lost time. They'd soon abandoned the ramblers' club in their home town of Biggar (too tame) and set off with their caravan in pursuit of Munros. Their tally so far was 190. Earlier in the week they'd traversed the seven peaks of the South Cluanie Ridge at a spanking pace in seven and a half hours. Expecting a leisurely descent, I accompanied them down to the inn and found myself in a race. The man was on his mettle and his legs, shorter than mine, went like pistons. I was hard pressed in keeping up. I shared a drink with them before driving to the end of the glen to buy a new map at the garage shop. I just made it before it closed for the night.

After a meal and a glass or two of Murphy's at the inn, my eyes began to close and I retired to my bunk in a cell at the back of the hotel and fell instantly asleep. Then the Murphy's took its toll. I jumped naked from the top bunk to go to the lavatory and was set upon by a squadron of midges, zooming in for blood through the open window.

From far and wide you can see the cairn on A'Chralaig, the

Creel, a monstrous thing built like a small broch. The morning was hot and hazy and by the time I reached the top I was sweaty. From A'Chralaig the route continues in a squiggly line along a ridge which starts off broad but narrows spectacularly approaching Mullach Fraoch-choire, the Hill of the Heathery Corrie. It gave me butterflies just to look at it, but tremors vanished with the hands-on experience (they usually do). Finding the rock conforming to the hand and solid underfoot, edging along ledges, wriggling through crannies and hoisting the body over rough obstacles, all with a sense of dizzy slopes on either hand – this salts and peppers any hill walk. But I shouldn't exaggerate. Kintail isn't the Cuillin, I'm no adventurer and the challenge was mild and mainly in my mind. All the same, I reached the Mullach pleased with my small exertions.

Where now? Back where I'd come? On to the challenging spike of Ciste Dubh, the Black Peak? But Ciste Dubh was a mile away with a deep glen intervening. On such a day, in such heat? – not to be endured. So I withdrew to a point where I could safely descend towards the watershed, where a lochan feeds two burns, one flowing northwards to Glen Affric and the other south into the Cluanie loch. What I'd not bargained for was the effect of hot sun in an airless corrie. It was a cauldron. Glassy pools in the burn looked inviting. No one was about; the nearest were a couple of tiny figures on the skyline, it was all mine. I found a mossy gorge overhung by two birch trees where the stream ran deep and slow over a paving of smooth rock and plunged into water so cold it took my breath away.

Sun-scorched, midge-bitten (they swarmed over my bathing pool), tired, thirsty and footsore, I crunched over the gravel path to the inn and an unexpected encounter.

'Hi John!'

The voice was familiar. Sitting in the bar window was Michael, an artist friend (two of his pictures hang in my flat), his wife Sheena, their son and daughter and various friends. The men had hired a week's fishing at Shiel Bridge and the families were visiting for the weekend.

'Come over, spend a couple of nights with us', he
urged. There was plenty of room, plenty to eat, and piping hot
water was on tap day and night from the big Aga stove. They loved
that Aga. Baths up to the neck, said Sheena. It was too tempting. I
decided to prolong my trip and stay with them the following night.

They left to stoke the mighty Aga and cook their meal and I
sat on watching the passing show in the bar. Gradually tourists and
trippers thinned out to be replaced by the ragamuffin trade from
the hills, some in shorts, others in tracksuit bottoms, feet still in
boots or eased into trainers, limbs and faces reddened by the sun,
hair in greasy tangles. A woman hobbled painfully – blisters or a
sprain, I don't know which. All around was chatter about how hot
it had been and what they'd climbed and Christ! that's a good pint,
aren't we ready for that. Later I exchanged a word to two with a
tall, stringy, grey-haired woman in her sixties, writing postcards in a
window corner. I commented on one, a view of a mountain range.

'Can you name them?' she challenged. She was one of those
formidable women I used to call county – posh accent (English,
Scot, Anglo, who knows?), dressed in sensible tweed well cut, ready
to put the world in order. No, I couldn't name her hills. She could
and did, for she'd climbed them all in a lifetime's walking. 'Winter
or summer', she said, 'my boots are ready'.

My boots were ready next day and the waiting ridge
shimmered in a heat haze – aptly, since Aonach air Chrith translates
as the Trembling Ridge. The summit is one of the seven South
Cluanie Munros which many walkers – like my Darby and Joan
from Biggar – traverse from one end to the other in a day. I was
happy with just a slice of it.

I left the road a mile from the inn and crossed tussocky
moorland towards a spur the Aonach flings out into the glen. On
another day I'd have gone straight for the ridge, avoiding the corrie,
in order to enjoy open views. But I was thirsty, dehydrated from
yesterday's walk and a pint too many afterwards, and I was tempted
to stick close to a friendly burn that purled through peat banks. I
drank often from its gushing spouts and it refreshed me on my way.

The time came to leave the Allt Coire nan Eirecheanach (outlandish name for a wee burn) and quit the corrie. I scrambled through outcrops on to the ridge, where I found tall stacks guarding the way to the mountain top. They could have been skirted but it was fun to clamber over them, and I was pleased with the airy exposure. This craggy line is off the beaten track and all the better for it. It's a little more adventurous, I believe, than any stretch on the seven-Munros-in-a-day trail. And to boot, you can follow straight on to the best part of the well-trodden route, the ridge leading to the adjoining Munro, Maol Chinn-dearg (Ginger Hill).

From there it was an easy walk to Sgurr an Doire Leathain, Peak of the Wide Thicket. No thicket now; I sat on its bald pate and looked down on a small disc of blue water, one of only two lochans to be found on the whole length of the traverse. This was the furthest point of my day. I returned to an intermediate peak called Sgurr Coire na Feinne, named for mythological heroes now absent from these parts, and then descended by the lumps and bumps of another ridge to a stalker's path that brought me neatly back to the road.

I turned my back on the Cluanie Inn and drove west. The lodge at Shiel Bridge is sheltered by trees and reached by a secluded lane. As I crossed the high-arched bridge I saw Michael knee deep in the water and mournfully casting for fish that weren't biting. At the lodge an apple-cheeked man and his black collie greeted me on the lawn, and inside I found another of the party with an opened half bottle of champagne on the table before him. He offered me a glass. Fizz at five on a sunny afternoon? Heck, yes.

Through mazy corridors and up the stairs, where I located a spacious room furnished with a bed, a dressing table, a writing desk and a vast wardrobe – good, solid old pieces all disfigured by a wash of primrose paint. The house had an air of neglected opulence. Handsome old furniture that had seen better days filled lounge and dining room, and old engravings hung on the walls – the Death of Patroclus caught my eye in the corridor, muscular young men in classical poses. Had this Homeric scene been provided for the pleasure of Edwardian house guests, or was it merely an item in a job lot bought to fill empty walls for the fishermen of today?

No doubt about the bath. It had the air of an original; sturdy, rotund, capacious and equipped with giant taps. But the water that spurted and thundered from the aged plumbing was not the steaming geyser I'd been led to expect. Alas, the Aga was in decline, starved of fuel and only able to deliver tepid water. The truth was that since the wives had returned to Glasgow on the bus leaving the men to their own devices, the place had gone to pigs and whistles. No one had stoked the stove. The choice for dinner, as Michael said when he arrived with his fish satchel empty, was to eat out or have cold scraps and leftovers. There was no debate. We sped back to the Cluanie Inn.

We were five at table, and numbers were growing. The latest arrival was a retired teacher, one of the old school of hill walkers who still puff on a pipe. That day he'd climbed the Saddle, a classic scramble. On returning to the lodge after our meal we found another car in the drive and two brothers installed in the house. John was planning an overnight fishing trip. Roderick, the younger one, was visiting from California where he earned his living by making period instruments – oboes and flutes for the new age of antiquity, one flute a week on average. He was also an innkeeper, though the inn turned out to be no more than a guest house – one of the few bed and breakfasts in the States – run by his wife and offering 'the comfort of a motel and the warmth of a home'.

We sat up late round the old deal table in the kitchen telling tales and drinking a few nightcaps. By the time I left the company to go to bed the level in the whisky bottles had fallen sharply. When I rose in the early morning the bottles were empty and no one was about. I sneaked out into the grey and misty dawn, crunched over the gravel and turned the car for home.

7

Hand in hand

From higher ground in Glen Coe the faint line of an old military road can be seen winding up to a pass. The Devil's Staircase, once a masterpiece of its kind, has deteriorated with the passage of time, winter weather and the tread of countless boots, so that now its causeyed surface is worn, shattered and gouged by floodwater channels. As I reached the pass a buffet of wind snatched my breath away and hurled stinging hailstones in my face. In less than an hour after that I'd dropped out of the wind, the sky had cleared and the sun was shining, and there were green trees by the wayside as I tramped the broad gravel track that leads to Kinlochleven.

Kinlochleven is a graceless village, built for an aluminium works with little regard for the beauty of its setting at the head of Loch Leven. The industrial buildings are grey and forbidding and most of the houses creosote-darkened timber lookalikes four in a block. People were about when I arrived, enjoying the late afternoon sunshine, clipping a hedge, talking, shopping. They don't see much sun. Squeezed in a valley between mountains, Kilochleven is shadowed for most of the winter.

My landlady was houseproud. I left dirty boots on the doorstep and still felt guilty at printing stockinged feet on her carpets. The bathroom was decorated all in shades of pink. Fluffy pink lavatory seat, pink bath, pink basin. I showered behind a pink curtain and emerged pink skinned. My landlady cooked at the school and she and her son had grown plump on school dinners. Supper began with soup, followed by a mountain of salad with new potatoes buttered and glistening in their jackets, and then the calories came in squadrons with pudding and sugary home baking.

There were two of us at table. My companion was small and slight, with blue eyes and a cascade of light brown hair round an elfin face.

'I'm Mary', she said.

Like me, Mary came from Glasgow and we discovered shared interests and people we both knew, like Edward McGuire the composer, flautist and member of the Whistlebinkies, and George, a fiddler and folkie who lived in the same block of flats as I did. We had a drink together in the village's one and only pub. Next morning I left her still at breakfast. I set off early, hoping to catch the midday train from Fort William, and waved to her over the hedge and the gnome, the mushroom and the windmill in the garden.

It was months before we met again and at first we didn't see a lot of each other. When we did, it wasn't to climb hills. We were both busy – she was a mature student at university and had two sons to look after. We ate at my flat sometimes. We went to the theatre, the opera, to concerts. The Glasgow Herald (as it was then, before Glasgow was dropped from the title) sponsored midweek concerts and guests were invited to supper with the conductor, soloists and some of the players. One night Mary sat beside the elderly cellist Paul Tortellier who stroked her thigh gently under the table, which in my opinion showed his good taste. Mary told me this with a grin; I think she rather fancied the old charmer. Madame Tortellier sat on his other side but whether she shared in the favours I don't know.

One summer day we drove into the green Lanarkshire countryside so that I could interview the artist Ian Hamilton Finlay. We sat outside the cottage in his garden of delights, an arcadia of groves and half-hidden statuary, and talked while doves fluttered over his rooftop.

The first hill we climbed together was in the Lake District, a curtain raiser for Macbeth. It was my year for Macbeths. In Berlin I'd seen a production at the Schaubühne – '*Ein grosser Flop*', as even the company spokeswoman admitted (though I liked it). Glasgow Citizens' set it in a nuclear winter, and I hated that. My third Macbeth was in Manchester, and Mary came too.

On the way south we gave ourselves time for a detour into

the Lakes, which Mary had never seen. We drank coffee at
Glenridding and started on Helvellyn. All went well till we left the
shelter of Glenridding Beck, aiming for Whiteside Bank and the
final ridge. Once we got on to the ridge with the summit in sight,
the wind blew the stuffing out of us. We battled on until Mary, hair
streaming in front of her eyes like a curtain, skittering about like a
leaf in the gale, gave a wail of distress. Small and light, she struggled
to make any progress. We turned and flew down wind-assisted by
way of the red-rocky desert of Raise.

The Royal Exchange in Manchester is theatre in the round,
built inside an Edwardian corn exchange (badly damaged a few
years after our visit in the IRA bomb blast). From our seats in the
front we could have leaned over and touched the actors. This
Macbeth took place in a Nazi concentration camp and the actors
wore prison pyjamas. The few props were made from found objects
– crowns were wire and broken glass, swords were strips of old
metal. The play ended when the theatre doors swung open and the
cast exited into bright light – going, we imagined, to their deaths. It
was an emotional experience and we sat in silence for minutes after
the actors had gone.

After the tragedy came bedroom farce. We'd booked into a
new hotel which seemed suspiciously cheap for a city centre. The
decor was a rare kitsch. A stuffed polar bear stood in the foyer with
a couple of stuffed alligators nearby ('What kind of a zoo have you
brought me to', said Mary). There were regency stripes, lacquered
chinoiserie, and English sporting prints in the corridors. Our room
was pitch dark, even when I drew back the curtains – no window!
Then the truth dawned (the only dawn that room would see).
Where the window should have been was a panoramic view of the
Manhattan skyline at night, in colour. In the morning we woke in
darkness, paid the bill and hurried home.

The spiny Aonach Eagach in Glen Coe is said to be the best
ridgewalk on the mainland, a length of some two miles 'irregularly
serrated and shot in places into spires', in the words of an

eighteenth century travel writer. Seen from below, the north flank of Glen Coe is a curtain of ravaged rock. The traverse is not for the unskilled, the unfit, or anyone whose stomach churns over a steep drop. The pinnacles can be dizzying, and in winter the hazards for walkers may be severe.

Mary and I had an experienced companion in Alan Thomson, photographer, climber and author of an excellent book on the glen and its hills. After a pelting start to the day the weather had improved slightly but it was gloomy overhead and there was rain in the wind. The forecast was not hopeful. We debated whether to go up.

Alan advanced the theory that it's better to start late, on the suspect principle that bad weather in the morning will usually clear later in the day. I think this is a rationalisation of his reluctance to rush breakfast. But this day the Thomson late start theory was vindicated.

We tackled the hill Am Bodach — whose summit marks the start of the ridge — head on, picking out a zigzag trail up the southern shoulder, an open route that enabled us to look across the glen at the black-bosomed Three Sisters on the other side. Alan set a fast pace and we struggled at his heels. He also talked a lot, as is his way. In the main the conversation was a monologue from Alan punctuated by a few breathless grunts from Mary and me. 'How does he do it?' she wheezed in my ear.

Thus, when the cairn emerged suddenly from the misty drizzle, we'd made excellent time. Should we continue? It seemed feeble not to finish the route, having put out so much energy on the preliminaries. We couldn't see the ridge unwinding ahead, but that, I thought, might be a blessing. If you can't see the drop you're not afraid of it. And though it was wet it wasn't windy, which was the deciding factor. With care, we'd not slip.

With Alan as pacemaker there wasn't time to dwell on difficulties. The thick mist began to lift soon after we started on the traverse, affording occasional glimpses of the long Blackwater reservoir on the right and down past rock buttresses into Glen Coe on the left. The ridge is relentless for most of its length. Rock pinnacles, slabby ledges and jagged crests uncoil mercilessly, forcing the walker to slot feet into crannies and constantly to use hands. All the time we had to take care not to let rucksacks snag or jar or bump us off balance.

After a couple of hours of hard labour we reached the summit of Sgorr nam Fiannaidh, the second of the Aonach Eagach's two Munros and the last peak on the ridge, and settled down on a shelf for lunch and a dram. The day had improved wonderfully. There were broad patches of clear sky and lying passively ahead of us the blue waters of Loch Leven opened out into the western ocean. Alan talked temptingly of Big Greenies – a local beer.

Coming off the heights, we ignored the track leading towards the frightening Stone Shoot and continued in the direction of the Pap of Glencoe. From a lower level the Pap is a graceful swelling but from this angle it showed merely as a rough tumulus, humble and not breast-like at all. Skirting to the west of it we picked up a path leading down to the glen and soon were crossing slopes where honey-scented heather brushed our boots and we could stop to pick blaeberries, little blue berries that left no more than a hint of sweetness in the mouth. We were in shirt sleeves now, the sun hot on our shoulders.

Where the hillside turned soggy I slipped and plumped down in squelchy moss, and had to continue clammy-arsed. 'Someone slips there every time', said Alan unhelpfully. But I was dry in no time, dry enough to sit in comfort in the Clachaig Inn and sink that Big Greenie.

I first knew Alan when we worked together in Glasgow on the now defunct Evening Citizen newspaper. I didn't know then that he was an outdoors man, and I certainly wasn't. I preferred to read a book, but Alan had been a keen cyclist from youth, and rock climbing had become his passion. We both left the Citizen to freelance, and he went to live near climbing country in a lodge at Ballachulish. There he practised photo-journalism, climbed to his heart's content, and joined the Glen Coe rescue team.

He's a warrior. When we were traversing the Aonach Eagach he told us about a car accident years ago in which he'd broken his neck. He was driving out of the glen when his car skidded on ice, shot off the road and somersaulted. Alan heard his spine snap and had the presence of mind to instruct helpers to keep him rigid when they got him out of the car. When he got to the hospital he overheard the doctor tell his assistants, sotto voce: 'He thinks he's broken his neck but he hasn't.' Alan knew better.

As soon as he could he signed himself out of hospital and proceeded to make a full recovery.

Some time after our walk he was winter climbing in the glen with a younger man. He was leading when the ice splintered and he fell fifteen feet, shattering the knee of one leg and breaking the ankle on the other. Wedged on a shelf of rock, in pain, he lay helpless. He and his friend flashed torches till help arrived in the early hours. Alan's wife, worried when he didn't return, persuaded his colleagues in the rescue team to turn out, and he was helicoptered off at four in the morning.

I called on him on my way back from walking in Ardgour some time later and found him hobbling with sticks and already back on a bike, doggedly exercising and determined to get back to the hills again. Which, of course, he did.

Buachaille means herdsman and there are two of them at the entrance to Glen Coe. Buachaille Etive Mor is the big one and Buachaille Etive Beag the smaller. Seen from the road they're a dour pair of sentinels, a first warning that this glen is not for Sunday strollers – at least, not the rocky front the Buachailles present. A late minister of the parish (last century) considered these heights 'accessible only to the eagle and his feathered friends', but that was before rock climbers got to work. Most routes up the face of the Buachaille, as the big one is familiarly known, are strictly for climbers, with walkers confined to the trodden path we took or, if adventurous, the famous Curved Ridge.

We'd started out with no clear object in mind. I had a vague notion of trying Ben Lui, the big alpine hill near Tyndrum, Mary had thought of its neighbour Ben Oss, but we were carefree. A fixed plan seemed unnecessary and possibly unwise, for the weather was unpromising. On leaving Glasgow we met a wall of fog. Loch Lomond was dismal in the half light of early morning; nothing was visible beyond the margin of the water. Two or three boats moored in the bay by Inchtavannach island sat motionless and shadowy, eery in in a oneness of still water and hanging mist. When the fog began to thin I pulled into the road-end at Dalrigh, just before Tyndrum, to waken my sleeping passenger and discuss tactics. Ben Lui rose massively out of a carpet of mist, with shreds of white in its big central corrie, a tempting prospect. But since the skies seemed to be brighter to the north we decided to drive on and take our chance on the Buachaille.

The white house of Altnafeadh was deserted that day, an empty shell with blackened beams where the roof had burned out. Ours was still the only vehicle to park there, a rare experience on a Sunday morning in Glen Coe. At nine we were stepping out across frosted grass. The route crosses the River Coupall by a high wooden bridge; the channel is wide but the water was low. Across the way the climbers' cottage Lagangarbh had been freshly painted; someone in the Scottish Mountaineering Club had been busy. The track soon enters the jaws of Coire na Tulaich, the breech in the mountain's seemingly impenetrable rampart that gives access to the highest point, Stob Dearg. A narrow and steepening path hugs the banks of the burn, almost dry that day. When the path forked we kept to the right bank which proved to be a mistake as it faded out and we had to climb into the gully, hop across the stony bed and claw our way up a slope mantled with heather to the better path on the other side. High up on the headwall of the corrie we clambered zigzag through bare red rock and rubble.

The air was clear and quiet in the calm of a frosty morning, but sudden sounds puzzled us, a sharp cracking and rattling we couldn't account for. It must have been the noise of frostbound

stones breaking loose and tumbling, freed by the rising
temperature. Nothing dropped in our vicinity, fortunately.
Unscathed, we scaled a rocky staircase to the broad, flaky back of
Stob Dearg's summit ridge.

At this height a frail, thinning mist still hung in the clammy
air, but the way to the top over advancing waves of red granite was
clearly signposted by a string of roseate cairns. We picked our way
over snow crystallised by the cold, walking into bright sunshine and
a strangely airless atmosphere. A faint breeze had touched our faces
and then died as we cleared the corrie edge, and not a breath, not a
zephyr kiss could now be felt. Calm weather on a mountain top is
rare. At 3,000 feet there's almost sure to be at least a featherlight
movement in the air, and to find such stillness in midwinter
astonished us. It was warm, too. The sun shone in a clear sky,
reflecting below us off waves of cottonwool vapours that filled the
glens and cast them into gloom, while we basked in the false
summer of the upper regions.

We reached the summit cairn and walked on to where
battered stone shelters perch like old fortifications on the lip of the
precipice, then ambled round the summit enjoying the peace and
isolation. Rannoch Moor lay invisible below the cloud level and
only the highest points poked through; the spiky tops of the
Mamores, the bulk of Ben Nevis, and closer, looking westwards,
burly Ben Starav.

So far we'd had the hill to ourselves, but now two walkers
approached. Both men had ice axes, a proper precaution in this
season. We'd been foolish and left ours in the car. More important,
for the moment, was that I couldn't find my glasses. Had I dropped
them? Reading a map would have been a problem without them,
but fortunately the route was clear and no navigating was needed.

Since the light would soon begin to fail we decided to cut
the day short by coming down the flank of the mountain. I
squinted at the map and surveyed the descent into the corrie as best
I could. There was scree to cross to begin with, then a steep slope
of grass, hard with frost. 'It's got a bane in it', said Mary – a phrase

of her father's, used when digging his potatoes out of frosty soil.

Here and there we skirted rocks sheeted with ice. But it was clammy in this airless pocket and since we kept up a fast pace all down the glen we arrived at the car bathed in sweat. I was glad to get changed. I was also relieved to find my glasses where I'd left them on the dashboard.

Not a trace of mist remained by the time we crossed Rannoch Moor, and as we approached Crianlarich, Ben More and Stob Binnein, with a dusting of white on their tops, stood out in the evening glow against a pearly sky. The luck didn't last. We reached the first bank of fog at the head of Loch Lomond and it wrapped us softly all the way back.

The Buachaille is a fine hill. A year later I hoped to return the but was cheated by the weather. That Christmas season was wild, and blizzards and a landslide between them closed the glen for a week. I stayed by the fireside.

Newly delivered logs were stacked by the door of Mary's flat when I called. It was the season for blazing fires and an armchair at the hearth.

We were off to Fort William. Once there, the wind blew up into a gale overnight and rain, hail and sleet beat a tattoo on the window pane of our hotel room. Morning light brought little cheer. Under a grey blanket of cloud the slopes formed a monochrome backdrop with none of the sparkle that even a hint of sunshine lends to a snowy landscape.

We took the sharp bend over the timber bridge half way along Glen Nevis and continued to the car park under the Ben. Three hardy souls were busy unloading their dormobile, intending to pitch tent overnight somewhere in the hills. We spoke to them in a flurry of snow and didn't envy them a bit. Our chosen route was to cross the river upstream where a footbridge was marked on the map, a skeleton thing known as the Wire Bridge (which we'd read about but never seen) and then attempt the steep slopes of An Gearanach, one of the Mamore peaks. We pulled on cagoules, overtrousers and leggings, shouldered our packs and axes and set off. A rugged track leads through a tangle of trees in a gorge, down which the tormented Water of Nevis thunders over a narrow bouldery bed. This wild place, according to one writer (name now forgotten by me) is 'almost Himalayan in character'. I can't vouch for that but it was awesome as we crunched along, snubbing toes on broken ground and fending off hanging branches and dripping foliage.

From the narrowest section of the gorge a spectacular view of the Steall burn tumbling down rocky shelves on the opposite hillside makes a dramatic background. Under this waterfall stands a white-painted climbers' hut, reached by the wire bridge which we were now required to cross. We'd been warned it wasn't for the faint-hearted and as we stood on the bank studying it I quailed. The wire bridge consists of three rusty hawsers stretched across the river, one below for the feet and two above for use as handrails. It struck me that the wire bridge had something of the aforesaid 'almost Himalayan' characteristics – I've read about shoogly bridges over tumbling cataracts in that part of the world. I clambered up, placed a foot on the quaking cable, gripped the rough wires in my gloved hands and inched out over the water. The bridge swayed with each step, the wind gusted and I began to feel groggy. The wires sagged in mid stream but at the far end, where the current cut into the high bank and the river flowed deep and green, they rose steeply and the transition from cables to terra firma looked as if it might be tricky. I paused and looked back. Mary had followed me on to the wires, and with her small frame spreadeagled she looked like a victim of the Inquisition on an instrument of torture.

She advanced a little and then stuck. 'I can't move', she cried.

'Go back', I shouted, glad of the excuse. I wasn't sorry to return, edging foot against foot back on to solid ground.

The wire bridge is the only practical way into the Mamores from the Nevis side and droves of climbers and walkers negotiate it in safety. We determined that one day, when conditions were better, when it wasn't so windy and when the water was lower and the banks dry, we'd pluck up courage and make the crossing – which I since have done, several times. What was the fuss about?

For the rest of the day we floundered. Having been balked of An Gearanach, the question was where to go. Indecision ruled, and we set off further up the glen with little idea of what to do. On our side of the burn the track went over a strip of flat ground bare of vegetation, other than rank grass, but on the far side trees dotted the lower slopes. Craggy, snowy hills, tops lost in cloud, formed a barrier wherever we looked. The snow, hard driven by the wind, drew a speckled veil across the landscape. Half a mile further on we stopped at the ruins of a croft house, consulted the map and decided to make for a ridge of Aonach Beag which hung in a rocky circlet above us. The snow lay deep and soft on the slopes and we made poor progress. Reaching the bluff marked on the larger scale Ordnance Survey map as An Teanga we stopped and surveyed the scene, wedging ourselves in between rocks for a bite to eat to restore our ebbing strength. Above our heads the clouds whirled around grey-black peaks. We were on the rim of a long, flat, snow-filled corrie through which a peat-brown river curled its way under white banks, serpentine and surprisingly wide, at least on that day. We thought of proceeding on to the high ridge which sprouts southeast from Ben Nevis, but the difficulty we foresaw in negotiating the burn and, worse, the sight of snow being whirled off the top and flung into space in ragged spirals deterred us. We turned back without regret.

At the car I took out the flask Mary had given me as a present (engraved on it the words of Burns, '. . . wi usquebae I'll face the Devil' – and maybe even the Wire Bridge, I thought), and we defied the Bad Man and his biting cold with the help of a large Glenmorangie. Malt whisky put the world in a better light. We'd been five hours on the hill and got nowhere, but we'd been companionable and cheery, and we drove back in jolly mood to the hotel, where we bathed, dined, and relaxed with the Sunday papers in a corner of the bar, eavesdropping on climbers with wind-burnished faces telling tall tales over their aggregating pints.

It snowed heavily in the night and was snowing still when we left the following morning. There was a thick covering on the road in Glen Coe and by the time we reached the exposed summit of Rannoch Moor I had to slow down to a crawl because of the drifting. But the skies had cleared and shafts of sunlight glinted and sparkled on a blinding landscape. The moor, tawny and speckled with blue water at other seasons, was a trackless white sea of undulating billows, ringed by snowy mountains. A benediction.

We had planned a weekend with others at Mamore Lodge, but it was touch and go. A domestic crisis kept Mary late and it was tea time on Saturday, a day in arrears, when we left Glasgow. It was a fine April evening, the road was quiet and there were clear views of snow-spattered peaks all the way from Balloch at the southern end of Loch Lomond till darkness fell at Glen Coe. We pushed open the bar door at the lodge to find the rest of the party round a sparking log fire, and wolfed supper of sausages and chips splashed with ketchup from a bash-on-the-bottom bottle.

Our room overlooked grounds with fine old trees round an overgrown pond. It was snug and the electric blanket was on. Because Mary liked to be read to and I like reading aloud we lay pillowed together and drowsed to an account of the 'Ascent of Ben Muich Dhui' from Queen Victoria's journal of her life in the Highlands: how the queen climbed Macdui on a pony led by John Brown with Albert walking at her side, how the wind at the top blew away the mist to give 'a dissolving view' of 'the grandest, wildest scenery imaginable', and how they searched for cairngorm stones on the plateau and found a few small ones. They'd look in vain now. Gemstone gatherers picked the slopes clean long ago.

The good weather held the following day. We took the familiar track into the corrie, the sheltered Coire na Ba, where it was mild and almost windless, and we soon cast outer clothes. Higher ground was covered in deep snow. We reached Stob Coire a'Chairn, a Munro and the central point of the arc enclosing the corrie, and looked hopefully towards broad-shouldered Am Bodach (the Mamores Am Bodach, not its namesake in Glen Coe), but there were a dozen in the party with varying experience and it seemed unwise to proceed along the narrow corniced ridge. Instead we turned towards the tall cone of Na Gruagaichean, where ice underfoot, thinly veiled in a light cover of snow, brought us to a halt on the rocky scramble just short of the summit. Rather than bother with crampons so near the top, the leader chipped steps up the last stretch. A circle of summits surrounded us. All cameras came out and there was much snapping of snowy hills.

Mary and I, needing to be home early, loped down the heathery brae, taking toll on our knees, and got to the lodge for a shower and a quick gathering of gear before the rest of the party arrived in time to wave us off.

Later Mary and I spent another night at Mamore Lodge on a December weekend of foul weather. A hurricane wind blew us off the ridge into Coire na Ba, clutching hands for safety. Hailstones – shotgun pellets – cut our cheeks and blinded our eyes, making the descent purgatorial. Once into the relative shelter of the glen there was a roaring and thundering so loud it sounded like a jet plane close up. It was wind in the trees alongside the burn, their branches whipped by the gale into screaming agony.

Next day brought peace, but also anti-climax. It was windless and the still atmosphere was laden with a thick, damp mist. Nothing could be seen beyond the immediate grey surroundings. We left with the intention of climbing Binnein Beag, one of the easternmost of the Mamores, but the enveloping blanket robbed us of the inclination once we found ourselves on the rim of grey water which could just be identified as Coire an Lochain. There was more than a mile to go and progress would involve painstaking map and compass work.

So we retraced our steps to a little cairn, just a few stones piled on top of each other, marking the start of a faint track leading up in the direction of Sgurr Eilde Beag (the Wee Hind's Hill), a spur of Binnein Mor. There was no track marked on the map and no way of knowing where it would take us in the end, but it seemed worth exploring. As we'd hoped, we reached Sgurr Eilde Beag and then followed the ridge past the south top of Binnein Mor and along the sharp, snow-crested approach to the big hill itself. Mary took my hand as we clambered together over the last bouldery yards to the cairn, where we celebrated our unpremeditated conquest of the highest peak in the Mamores. Visually there was nothing to toast; the view, such as it was, being a screen of white, black and shades of grey.

We pored over the map looking for a possible descent from the saddle between Binnein Mor's nameless south top and Na Gruagaichean. The contour lines were tightly bunched but it seemed practical. A layer of wet snow lay treacherously on the steep grassy headwall of the corrie, but we took it slowly and got down in comparative comfort. The slopes of Sgurr Eilde Beag, once they became visible under the raft of mist, were streaked with welts of sunless snow and contrasting black rock and heather.

We had a good Christmas. Mary cooked dinner for her extended family (she was one of eight children). Her elderly neighbour hobbled arthritically downstairs, sat in a chair and sang Scots songs. Mary had been good to him. She'd listen to his tales of road walking in the depression years, and often she'd shop for him. Later that year when she was ill she rested on his sofa and he tried to cheer her. He called her 'my wee darling'.

At the year's end, on Hogmanay, she came to my flat for 'the bells', the chimes that ring out the old year and ring in the new. Close by, the croaky carillon in the Tron tower played wobbly hymns and carols. Sitting at table over supper we toasted the new year, then poked our heads through the skylight window to watch fireworks cascade over Glasgow Green and hear the rusty strokes of midnight.

8

The year that's to come

On January 1 we walked through Scots pines, dark green against the tawny grass, on our way to Ben Oss. I'd never heard of Ben Oss till Mary first mentioned it. Oss lurks out of sight of the road north, overshadowed by its flamboyant neighbour Ben Lui.

Another hill-walking friend of Mary's had tried to warn her off. 'Don't let him take you in winter', he said. 'It's a complicated hill'. Well, I wasn't going to have that. (Own up: I was jealous. He was a rival).

So we duly tramped up the corrie beside a burn which carved small gorges into the hillside, encrusted in the higher reaches with snow and hanging icicles. At this height we were in fog and had to find our way by compass on to the broad bealach that links Oss and its neighbour Beinn Dubhchraig. Once there we slithered on glassy ice and had to turn back, since Mary didn't have crampons. From then on Oss became our bête noire. We made several more vain attempts on it, together or singly.

We had better luck with Stob a'Choin a few days later. Seen from Inverlochlarig in Balquhidder, claimed to be the site of Rob Roy's house and a favourite starting point for Stob Binnein and Cruach Ardrain, it has a rugged aspect. Stob a'Choin, the Dog Peak, is not on the Munroists' hit list and many walkers ignore it. There are higher peaks in this neck of the glen. But if it lacks size it has a serrated skyline which zigzags erratically and temptingly hither and yon and up and down. In mist it could be a real test of navigation. When we set out after pelting rain, shafts of pale sunlight gave a faint hope of a fine day, and though most of the time the tantalising blue was obscured by scudding cloud and sudden squalls, and black storm veils shifted continually over the neighbouring tops, we had clear visibility when it mattered.

A chorus of barking dogs greeted us at the farm, and also a

pungent smell of dung. The footbridge over the Larig burn had been a fine one in its day, but that day was over. The handrail stopped short of safety, planks were missing and those that remained were greasy. Between the gaps we saw the river gliding black and sullenly below.

There's no path on the other side, so with the whole hillside to choose from we made a direct assault on the ridge. Near the top we heard a high-pitched cry in the crags, and then a shepherd appeared, a young man in duffle coat and welly boots, calling his dogs. He seemed mildly surprised to find us there rather than on the popular hills. One of the collies bounded joyfully over to us to have his ears scratched, while his master told us he had a thousand sheep on the hill, 27 of them rams which had been with the ewes and which he was now attempting to round up. So far he'd only located a dozen. One might be over there, he said, pointing to a few white specks on a far slope. Having asked us not to disturb any sheep on our way, he cut across the hill and we continued.

A short scramble through a cleft in the crags, which had us grabbing handfuls of sodden turf, brought us into the wind, rain and snow. Suddenly we were in the eye of a blizzard, mercifully brief. We quailed and bent our heads against the flurries, seeking a crag to shelter behind. The snow came in a solid gale, blinding us with sharp pellets. We staggered on, and I glimpsed featherlight Mary, buffeted, reaching for support from one of the rusty stanchions that once had carried a fence along the ridge. Once in the lee we watched the myriad flakes being hurled over the crest. And then, within a quarter-hour, it was over and we were back on course, treading the thin new coverlet of snow in a patch of stray sunshine. We'd crossed into a temperate zone. It was almost balmy. Mary admitted that she'd been on the point of suggesting we turn back. 'I'm glad we didn't', she said.

We passed the ruckle of stones that serves as a cairn without stopping. We had intended to return along the ridge, choosing another way down. But our way had proved so exposed that we changed plan and descended there and then on a slope sloppy with new snow, into a gully which brought us to open ground near the bridge. There we met our shepherd again. Two more rams had been found and he reckoned he knew roughly the whereabouts of another. Twelve to go.

We left him still traversing the slopes and as dusk gathered, braved the barking dogs, breathed afresh the aroma of the byre, and made all speed for the Rob Roy Inn at the foot of the glen.

The wind blew, the snow fell, and so did Mary, a tumbling head-over-heels on a thin cover of wet snow. No serious damage was done, fortunately.

We had started off on the wrong foot. Heading for Tarmachan, a hill near Ben Lawers, I turned right too early and drove along Loch Earn instead of Loch Tay. It was pelting all the way and when we eventually arrived at the Lawers visitor centre it had turned to snow. The car park was packed and there was a throng of skiers and walkers. We crossed under the dam where panels of ice had formed on the boggy ground and decided to tackle the slope head on. The crags are steep and in these conditions, with a partial coating of soft snow on rock ledges already festooned with grass and tuggy heather we had to be cautious. There was a blast of wind and a flurry, and when I turned to speak, Mary wasn't there. She was a blue bundle twenty feet below. She'd fallen, silently, somersaulting on the slope as she went, and plumped finally into a drift.

Two men and a dog passing below got to her first, picked her up (the dog Corrie licking her ears) and ascertained that there were no broken bones. They just happened to be members of the Killin mountain rescue team and since they'd come on an accident they proceeded to put their rescue techniques to the test. First they slipped Mary into a harness and clipped her on to a rope, then turned her to face the slope and brought her down backwards. Meanwhile Corrie, a collie with speaking eyes and a grizzled snout, gave enthusiastic support – tail wagging, bark, bark. On the way down they entertained us with stories of other accidents, most of

them fatalities. On Ben More the previous week a climber caught
in an avalanche had been skewered by his axe. Once they'd been
called out twice in twenty-four hours. One of four dead in those
incidents was a girl whose skull was empty as a cracked eggshell.
Her brains lay strewn on the rock beside her.

In this jolly vein we continued back to the car park, Mary
hobbling. She believed she'd been plucked off the slope by the
wind, but I suspected her boots. The plastic boots I wore were rigid
and safe on treacherous ground, and I'd assumed hers were equally
secure. She ached from some days afterwards and I suffered too,
from bruised pride. I felt my judgment had been at fault. I'd chosen
a bad route.

There's a stone school at the top of the village of Ballachulish,
close to the kirk. It was Saturday morning and I parked in the
empty playground. The sun was shining, a man mowed his lawn, a
dog barked.

Mary and I followed the lane past the farm into open
country, where it tracks over turf along the valley of the River
Laroch and then forks to give a choice of routes through the forests
which surround Beinn a'Beithir. There was new April snow on the
heights.

Beinn a'Beithir (or Thunder Hill, 'perhaps from the singed
red appearance of its two-pointed pinnacles', according to the 1841
New Statistical Account), is the generic name for a horseshoe range
of several peaks that sweeps round Ballachulish at the mouth of
Loch Leven. Our intention was to tackle it by the eastern or skyline
ridge which makes a sharp and rocky silhouette just above the
village. The prospect of having to scramble a bit appealed to us.

The approach is steep, and warm as we were, pausing from
time to time to catch breath or drink water, we gained height
quickly as the ridge narrowed from broad backed and turf
upholstered to sharp and rocky. Black forests in morning shadow
cloaked all the lower slopes to the south and east. The triangular
outline of the village hugged the loch with, seawards, the spidery

outline of the bridge crossing the narrows. Below us two tiny figures inched along the riverside track with a hyperactive dot of a dog coursing around them.

We encountered snow, a few isolated patches at first in the lee crevices and then more general cover, two or three inches deep on average but soft and wet and showing signs of a rapid thaw. It glistened in the sunshine and melted in threadlike rivulets over the hanging rock. On either hand the hillsides rose in steepening walls, the corrie on our right forming a bowl in which sparse trees in early leaf straggled beside a burn. The ridge now reared above us in a series of rock stumps, and we had to use our hands. I looked back and saw Mary clambering gamely over a ledge with the sweep of the glen foreshortened below her. She was agile in spite of her lack of reach.

Then we reached an obstacle slippery with snow and with no easy way round.

A small voice beside me: 'I can't go on'. I didn't demur. I think the fall on Tarmachan had unnerved her. Not wanting to abandon the hill entirely, we decided to cross the corrie to the gentler ridge opposite. Descending to better ground we started to pick a way just above the trees, through rocky outcrops, scree and snow patches. We came out on the ridge just beyond the point called Beinn Bhan, at about 2,000 feet. This ridge had a path on it and it was broad as a motorway compared to what we'd first attempted. It took us easily over broken rock to the top of Sgorr Bhan, where a young couple and an older woman − mother, presumably − were eating sandwiches at the cairn.

The ridge between Sgorr Bhan and Sgorr Dhearg, the first and higher of Beinn a'Beithir's two Munros, is a classic under snow. It curves upwards gracefully in a curling wave frozen in time. Two figures appeared on Sgorr Dhearg and began the descent towards us, covering the ground with surprising speed − possibly the snow gave a false impression of distance. As for us, we were content to rest on our laurels. The traverse of the corrie had been tiring and it felt as if we'd already climbed two hills rather than one. We descended, passing the young couple and mother on stony ground where the man's trainers seemed inadequate. His feet must have been wet and sore.

We lingered over Sunday breakfast in Glen Coe and even considered being tourists for a change. Maybe there was a museum to see? But the day had dawned bright and the hills were inviting. As a compromise we settled for the Pap.

There was snow on the high tops but the Pap, being a Tom Thumb among giants, pointed only a bony nipple to the sky. The Pap of Glencoe – Sgorr na Ciche, to give its Sunday name – is a true little mountain. All around are Munros but the Pap doesn't even make 2,500 feet. It's none the worse for that. It goes straight up in a no nonsense way, steeply enough to put legs and lungs to the test, and it's defended by a barrier of crags up which you may scramble if you desire, though there are tracks.

It doesn't much matter which starting point is chosen. There's only one way to go: look up and make for the top. We took the back road towards the Clachaig Inn and went through a wicket gate at the edge of woodland. Primroses peeped from mossy banks and gean trees were white with blossom. The path went by a stream gushing over rocks in a cleft, guarded by birch trees still bare. At a green sill in the hillside the tributary we followed took a sharp turn and disappeared in boggy ooze. Instead of spouts of water singing over stone there were suddenly only stagnant puddles mantled with green weed.

The grassy slope changed to heather and then to fields of rubbly rock. We heaved ourselves over riven blocks (some of the rock too crumbly for comfort) on to the round, slabby summit. From the cairn there were hazy views. Loch Leven lay at our feet, disfigured by the cages of a fish farm. Now and then a tiny car threaded its way along the twisting lochside road. Northwards were the snowy Mamores, with Ben Nevis hunched beyond them. Westwards the Coe river dribbled through the sands of its delta and beyond that the line of Ballachulish bridge and the sandy shores of Onich were just visible in the thickening distance.

We left our stony perch reluctantly. It was still only one o'clock when we squeezed through the gate, ready for lunch and a leisurely drive home. It had been a splendid morning, and to cap it all, on a sunny spring Sunday when the rest of Glen Coe was peppered with walkers and climbers, we'd had the hill to ourselves.

Just at the start of Glen Coe, behind the White Corries ski station, the big hill Creise boasts what the Munro book describes as 'a fine steep ridge'. This ridge takes the eye abruptly up to an eminence called Sron (meaning snout) na Creise.

Cross the River Etive, says the book, with the qualification that in spate it may be unfordable. Mary and I looked down on the Etive where it ran some yards wide through a deep gully. We were not eager, and came to the conclusion that we'd find a better chance of crossing dryshod upstream, where a cataract (if that's not too grand a word for it) of red rock cubes forces the water into channels narrow enough to be jumped.

I went first and Mary started to follow, but halted midstream on a boulder, wary of her next move. I came back to offer her a hand and she hopped over safely, whereupon I lost my footing and fell bottom down into the river. Thus a wet-arsed start to the day. The sun was shining and I steamed gently and soon dried. It didn't shine for long. The sky clouded over and it became chilly, and Mary changed her shorts for trousers. On the ridge we took one or two diversions from the path in order to clamber up rock, once reaching an overhang which forced us back, feeling blindly for footholds. From there it was only a step to the Sron.

Crouched behind the cairn for shelter, eating his sandwiches, was a man who became our companion for the rest of the day. A tall, lanky-legged, lean man in a red ski cap pulled over his ears, he envied us our sporting route – having come up tamely himself from the ski car park on the other side.

The true summit of Creise isn't easy to judge, and the Ordnance Survey makes a guessing game of it. We fixed on the northerly of the two tops, which are about a quarter of a mile apart. Another peak, Clach Leathad, rears up at the south end of the ridge with a sheer corrie wall cut into it, on this day overhung with a wicked snow cornice. According to our new friend, who seemed to be knowledgeable about such things, Clach Leathad had once been classed as a Munro until stripped of its title when the authorities who determine such arcana had second thoughts. It's high enough, no doubt about it.

We headed down to a bealach and then up a sharp, rising ridge which became steep and rocky at the top, to Meall a'Bhuiridh, the Roaring Hill (roaring as of stags), which was our second Munro of the day though we weren't aware of it at the time. We clambered up the last crags talking about travel. I'd just been to Tbilisi in Georgia where, from a distance, I'd seen the Caucusus.

'You should read Mummery', said our companion (Alfred Frederick Mummery, Victorian climber, writer of My Climbs in the Alps and the Caucasus, died 1895 on Nanga Parbat in the Himalayas). I'd never heard of Mummery, but when the name Richard Burton – not Richard Burton the actor but Richard Burton the Victorian explorer – cropped up in the conversation I was on familiar territory. This Burton, soldier, scholar and unsuccessful seeker after the source of the Nile, was featured in a recent film I wanted to see. It was set in Africa and called Mountains of the Moon.

'Boys Own Paper stuff', said our man, who'd just returned from a spell as a diplomat in Kenya. 'But you'll like the scenery'. As it happened the film, when I caught up with it, was a great disappointment – and so was the scenery.

A shock awaited us on Meall a'Bhuiridh. Suddenly we were entangled in a web of ironmongery, an unsightly jumble of rusting ski pylons with a scattered encampment of shanties below them – all the more wretched for being deserted at this season. We made our way down and the stranger drove us back to our car in Glen Etive. I asked his name – it was John Johnson.

Months later I read an article in a mountain magazine in

which the writer described his feelings towards the end of climbing the Munros. He'd got 276 in the bag but was strangely reluctant to add what was then the last one (more have been added since), not wanting to write finis to the story. In the course of the article he mentioned climbing the great peaks of Africa. The writer's name was Sir John Johnson, chairman of the Countryside Commission, former diplomat. Our man on Creise.

For days Mary had been listening to the forecast and she predicted a heatwave. 'It starts today', she said.

Saturday. Caravans were out in force. Tourists were strolling in shorts and sun tops when we bumped over the bridge across the Nevis river. It was hot already.

The Devil's Ridge offers 'a narrow arête, an airy climb up to the very exposed crest', according to Munro book. But first there was the stiff ascent up tussocky slopes and a stalker's path to Sgurr a'Mhaim (the Pointy Tit). There were faint, ringing shouts from above, and then two flocks of sheep appeared, driven by scurrying collies and two shepherds. Later, looking back down the glen, we saw the sheep spread over the green valley and packed into pens at the spot marked on the map as Sheep Wash.

Hairpin turns in the path took us to stonefields sparkling pink and white, Sgurr a'Mhaim's quartzite dome.

'So that was the Devil's Ridge', said a young man who'd followed us to the top with his girl friend.

'No it wasn't', said I.

Nothing would convince him. 'It says so here', he insisted, stabbing the map.

Suddenly, for no reason, the argument became rather heated, a total absurdity. We gave each other black looks and parted huffily, a strange spat on a hilltop.

'I was afraid you were going to hit him', said Mary when we were out of earshot.

Drifts of mist at first obscured and then revealed the adjacent peak of Sgor an Iubhair (then a Munro, but no longer), linked to the hill on which we stood by a narrow ribbon of undulating rock, the authentic and only Devil's Ridge. Bearing in mind the book's warning we gingerly approached Stob Choire a'Mhail, a steep little crest that rises challengingly in mid course. Three young cropped roundheads – I took them to be soldiers – slithered down an angled slab as we arrived, nodded to us and set off at a trot as soon as their feet touched the ground. We surmounted the slab with no great difficulty, and since it proved to be the most testing part of the ridge we concluded that the devil had been in a kindly mood when he created it. No doubt it presents a greater challenge in bad weather.

On Sgor an Iubhair, which is nominally the Peak of the Yew Tree though it's bare of any tree at all, we met a grey-haired walker in old-fashioned black boots who said he was on his second round of the Munros. It had taken him thirty years to finish the first, and he hadn't meant to when he started. After fifteen years he'd climbed fifty, at which stage he decided to speed up and knock them off. He started on a detailed catalogue of his climbs from which we were saved by the arrival of the young couple. No one mentioned the Devil's Ridge now. I gloated in secret.

Now the sun returned, bathing the tops and building up heat in the corries. Below us sparkled a deep-set lochan so greeny-clear and tempting that we descended and skinnydipped in it. We were in the centre of an arena, with a curtain of fluted rock curving round Iubhair to the snow-white quartzite flanks of Sgurr a'Mhaim. Anyone above might have had a grandstand view as we stripped and waded in over the shallow stony bottom. The water was cold. A quick dunk, a few hasty strokes and we stumbled back on shore, shivering.

The burn issuing from this lochan dashes through a narrow gully. We followed the path beside it and saw where the burn spouted into a smooth scoop of rock like a Jacuzzi. Once again we stripped, and sitting side by side on the rim, dangled feet in the water before summoning the courage to plunge in – but briefly. Then we dried off thankfully in the heat of the sun.

We walked on through a dying birchwood. Mingled with the live trees were as many dead; bare poles leaning drunkenly, or splayed on the ground among foxgloves, encrusted with moss. One survivor lay on its side with green leaves still sprouting from twisted branches, showing white wood where it had snapped in two in the last gale.

At night we dined at a hotel beside Loch Linnhe. The sun's last rays made a golden ladder across the surface, and silhouetted the serrated crest of Garbh Bheinn across the water in Ardgour – another tempting hill, though not for this trip.

There was a thin haze on Sunday morning. We were staying at a guest house run by the Weirs – Peter, a climber himself, later manager of the Glencoe ski lift, and his wife Rosemary.

'Give us a route, Peter', we said. 'Something scrambly'.

He gave us Dinner Time. From the window we could see the scarred north face of Aonach Dubh, the last of Glen Coe's Three Sisters. Peter pointed out the cleft we should follow, with a warning not to stray on to the rock climbing territory alongside.

So, Dinner Time. At the white farm cottage by Loch Achtriochtan we passed a man and tractor, and gave him a wave. The path grew fainter over a deepening gorge, the rock grew wilder, shattered, calling for agility here and there. Looking back we saw where Loch Leven merged into a murky haze – a change coming in the weather? Ahead the last bouldery gulch led on to a bare backbone. We were nearly there and it wasn't yet twelve noon. Dinner Time! More like lunch time. Elevenses, even.

But we were too cocky.

From the head of Dinner Time a stony ridge leads to the sentinel peak of Stob Coire nan Lochan, and behind it the higher summit of Bidean, one of the Glen Coe giants. There should have been vistas but something had definitely happened to the weather, and a dark mantle shrouded the longer views. A gloom hung over Ballachulish way and the waters of the loch were leaden. As we passed weird pillars and gaping gullies guarding the corrie on our left the pale sun gave up and slipped finally behind veils of mist. We reached the cairn in a shroud, and a keen rising wind forced us into the shelter of a rocky nook where we ate and drank with chilled fingers, huddled in windproofs, mitts and woolly hats. Some heatwave – one scorcher and already it was gone. There was no sign of Bidean and we'd lost any desire to reach it. Now came the rain, big drops that blotched the stones at our feet.

We descended towards the small lochans that give the Stob its name. From the saucer in which the lochans nestle the ground falls sharply in grassy slopes seeded with stones and boulders and veined with many rivulets. The rain fell in torrents, making the ground splashy and treacherous.

I fell, sat down rather, having slipped on a wet stone when chattering and not observing where I put my feet. A leg twisted under me and there was – could it be? – a thin snapping sound, then a sudden wrench of pain. I sat disconsolately in a puddle for a bit, cursing silently, then got to my feet and tested the ankle gingerly. It was painful. With luck it might be only a sprain. Finding I could hobble, I set off at a snail's pace, hopping at times, sitting down at the worst bits and inching over rocks on my backside.

We made for a track which snaked down into the glen far away. This path is steep and zigzags. It's narrow, rough and rocky. Even on two good legs it's a trial. We looked for a stick to help me but this hill is timberless, not a root, branch or even stout twig to be found. Hope came and went with a man who tapped his way past with the aid of a sturdy walking stick, just the thing. But he was fat, elderly and making heavy weather of it, and I reckoned his need was as great as mine. I didn't want two of us lamed. It took hours to get down and it was teatime before we reached the car, after a short welcome lift along the last half mile of road from a Samaritan in a Sierra.

It must have been a quiet Sunday evening at the Victoria Infirmary in Glasgow, for a line-up of doctor and nurses was waiting as I was wheeled along the corridor. 'Where's the band?' I asked. They cooed happily over the X-rays – the ankle was broken

– and put on a plaster up to the knee. A passing doctor asked cheerily if I'd read Touching the Void, Joe Simpson's book about an amazing adventure in the Peruvian Andes when he crawled down a mountainside with a shattered knee after falling into a crevasse. This, I thought, was a bit over the top.

A truck arrived to pick up the car and the teenage truck driver sportingly offered me a lift home to save the taxi fare. Rather than hurt his feelings I accepted. A mistake – the cab of a low loader is a long way from the ground and very difficult to get into backwards, with crutches, and a leg encased in plaster. Getting out was worse.

I hopped about my kitchen preparing supper like Long John Silver in his galley. Then I peeled off my trousers and lay in a hot bath with the stookie leg dangling over the side to keep it dry. Lug me to bed and let me sleep.

The heatwave came and went. It resumed on the Monday and for the next six weeks the sun shone from morning till night and no rain fell. For the rest of that glorious summer I languished. I didn't set foot on a hill. The sun streamed into my attic flat, always full of light, and the best I could do was study maps, read books and discuss future climbs with Mary.

It was 1990, Glasgow's year as European city of culture, and I had plenty of work to do covering the theatre, art and music for my newspaper. At last, after my usual stint in Edinburgh for the festival, when I hobbled round the capital with a stick, I put on trainers in preference to boots and headed with Mary and my younger son Adam for the Trossachs.

Little Ben An has all the attributes of a major peak except height and scale. Ben An is a mountain in miniature and anyone can be a mountaineer on it, which is part of its appeal. Woodland, rocky top, long views – it's got the lot. We passed through the Rob Roy village of Aberfoyle, messy with trippers, and drove through shaggy forest over the Duke's Pass. It was late in the morning and on other outings I'd have been fretting at the delay, but that day it didn't matter. We'd reach the top in no time, and besides, this was just a test-piece for fitness.

The Trossachs is tourist country and a signpost at the car park near Loch Achray points to the start of the ascent. A purist would scoff at the manicured path – walls to shore it up, sleepers over boggy ground, rough steps hacked out on the steeper inclines.

Red spotted toadstools big as saucers – fly agaric, the poisonous *Amanita muscaria* – sprouted on the verge of a shady ditch. Said Mary: 'Where's the pixie on top of the toadstool?'

The stony path, neatly corseted here and there, wound through birch, beech and ash, and the sun shone patchily through foliage still green before the onset of autumn. Soon the path joined a burn that chattered over stones, filling the air with a whiff of moist soil and dank vegetation. Adam, newly returned from working for a spell in the south and glad to be back, sniffed approvingly. 'It even smells better than England', he said.

Broadleaf trees gave way to conifers and then to open views of heather-tufted slopes, broken by choppy grey waves of outcropping rock. Beyond that rose the symmetrical cone of our friendly peak, for another of Ben An's modest virtues is that it doesn't deceive. What you think is the top is the top, not just a stage on the way. The track led through peaty turf and then up steep rocky ground, finally twisting round to the bouldery summit. Three rock climbers were on the crags. We'd seen them laying out their ropes and gear in the car park when we arrived and now we saw them spun out on a face just short of the summit.

'Is this it?' asked Mary in surprise as we emerged at the top. She was accustomed to harder labour. To mark the successful conclusion of my first post-ankle ascent we wedged a bottle in the summit rock and drank a toast to my recovery.

We were joined by a man and his dog. The man wore cut-off welly boots, the dog was a brown and white spaniel bitch, and both were Ben An veterans. He lived close by and climbed it regularly to keep fit, and the spaniel kept him company. I had my ankle, he had his hip, and we swapped case histories. Earlier that year he'd been

loping down this hill when a jaywalking rambler stepped into his
path. Swerving to avoid a collision he tumbled head over heels into
the burn. He'd torn muscles and dislocated his hip, but it didn't stop
him going on an Alpine holiday with friends six weeks later.

On the way down Adam forged ahead, Mary followed, and I
straggled. The ankle had begun to nag. We decided to visit the
Trossachs Hotel, a grand, grey granite, Scots baronial pile. There was
no one behind the bar, dungeon dark in the interior, and the
gloomy ballroom where a few couples sat dolefully round tables like
sad wallflowers, with their drinks before them, was mournful in
comparison with the sundrenched world outside. The hotel, as we
might have guessed, was living a half life. Built in the 1820s, its
many bedrooms were closed by damp. Dank and drear, it could
have been the setting for a gothic horror film (in better days it had
featured in a film of the Thirty-nine Steps). It has since been
renovated and made into time-share flats.

We moved on to the Loch Achray Hotel where we were
served by a sullen waitress (another blow for Highland hospitality)
and were buzzed by wasps as we sat outside with our beer. Other
wasps congregated in clouds over an elderly departing bus party,
causing them to break into a sudden creaky dance.

The long hot summer ended and we – the three of us again
– tackled Tarmachan in a different clime. Clambering up from the
dam we passed the spot where Mary had fallen in snow earlier that
year. No wonder, we thought when we saw the slope. We loped
along the famous little ridge which is twisting and lumpy and
briefly sharp, hurrying to keep a biting wind at bay.

It was on the way back from a hill that Jürgen made his brief
entry into my life. I'd taken Mary home and as I slowed down near
my flat in the Merchant City a young man dressed in suit and tie
tapped on the window. He asked in excellent English with a slight
German accent where he could get a bus. Earlier in the day his
coat, wallet and passport had been stolen in a Sauchiehall Street
pub. He had to get back to his lodgings in Baillieston, a big housing

scheme on the outskirts of the city, where he was staying with a friend.

I sighed. He looked upset and his story had the ring of truth about it. Having been robbed of everything in a Barcelona street the year before, I knew what he must be feeling. The simplest thing was to drive him to his friend's. As we turned into High Street he realised that his keys were missing, too, and his friend wouldn't be home till late. Not to worry, he said, he'd wait. In the dark? In the rain? On a pavement in Baillieston? I turned the car and drove to my flat.

He appreciated the meal I cooked.

'You like cooking?' – I said yes.

'I'll send you a German cookery book when I get back. That's a promise'.

In the next few hours I learned a lot about Jürgen. He sold life insurance and he was so good at it that if all went well he'd be able make enough to buy a small hotel when he was in his forties – 'You need a dream'.

After dinner he began to worry about his friend's house, since the address had been in his wallet and the thief would have the key. I drove him to Baillieston and parked just beyond the police station in the main street while he ran back to check on the house. Then we crossed to a pub where I bought him a pint and some cigarettes.

'Life', he said, inhaling, 'is beginning to feel better'.

At half-past ten I rose, bought him a farewell drink and said I had to leave. It shouldn't be long before his friend returned.

He touched my arm. Perhaps, he suggested diffidently, I could lend him enough money to get to the German consulate in Edinburgh for a new passport. Couldn't he tap his friend? – His friend was unemployed and broke. I lent the money.

Next day was Monday. At noon he turned up at the Herald office dressed in jeans.

'You see, I've kept my promise', he said, and handed me a school cook book in German.

But there was a snag. He hadn't been able to get a new passport as he needed security clearance – something about his national service – and for that he had to go to the embassy in London. I lent him the fare. He'd return the lot by Friday at the latest.

On Tuesday I mentioned Jürgen to a colleague who told me that the previous week he too had been approached in the street by a suave German speaking fluent English who'd begun by asking directions and ended with a request for money. I phoned the police and then the German consulate in Edinburgh.

'Ja, ja, we know that name', said the woman on the phone. 'It has cropped up over the past two years and always in a negative way. I am sorry. There are bad apples'.

Friday came but Jürgen did not. On Sunday morning, as I prepared to leave on holiday, the phone rang. It was Jürgen.

'Where are you?'

'I'm in Germany'. He seemed jaunty and prepared to chat, but I thought it was time to mention cash.

'I've posted it to you', he said.

It never reached me. Later that year I was summoned on a rainy night to an identity parade at Maryhill police station, with nineteen others who had befriended the plausible Jürgen (most of whom had parted with money). I picked him out immediately behind a one-way screen. He looked young and vulnerable and strangely I felt sorry for him.

I was eager to tell Mary the latest about him. He was to appear in court the following week and I intended to find out what happened. But by that time fate had banished Jürgen from my mind.

9

The climb's done

The Whangie is a nursery for climbers. The Whangie is a deep cleft in rock in the Kilpatrick hills north of Glasgow. The legend is that the devil whacked the rock clean in two in a fit of anger (Scots for a blow like a karate chop is a 'whang'). So the deil in a rage opened up a handy practice ground for apprentice climbers. Generations of rock climbers in the west of Scotland have learned their craft there.

Jim O'Donnell, a fellow journalist now turned printer (he printed this book), offered to give Mary and me our first lesson. Jim had been a keen climber until he acquired a wife, a family, a mortgage and a waistline. He was keen to get back on rock.

From the Whangie's inner sanctum Mary and I looked up at gnarled walls. They terrified me. Jim introduced us to the terminology. A 'difficult' route is easy, a 'V–diff' (for very difficult) is easy but not so easy as difficult, 'severe' is a shade more difficult. That's as far as we got. Then he disappeared above with a hank of rope, ran it round a solid rock at the top, dropped both ends over the edge and returned. Mary and I in turn attached ourselves to one end and attempted to scale as best we could while Jim on the other end acted as counterweight and took in the slack. Twice we came off and swung like a pendulum, but on the whole it was an encouraging start.

Jim was self taught. He'd been roaming the Kilpatrick hills, Ben Lomond and the Cobbler since boyhood. He and his climbing partner – also a journalist, now big on the Guardian – learned the craft by trial and error and reading descriptive books by such as Joe Brown and Don Whillans. They are credited with making a route on Pillar Crag, near Carbeth on the back road from Glasgow to Loch Lomond, which they christened Manky Crack (manky means dirty) because they had to dig out so much vegetation on the way. Climbers call this gardening.

About this time I picked up a second-hand copy of a book by
Frank Smythe, one of the great British climbers before and just after
the war, and for a while Smythe became bedtime reading for both
Mary and me.

A sample of Smythe in the Alps:'Just when everything
appeared hopeless, I saw a little ledge, a narrow gangway threading
the precipice. I stepped across it. The ledge broadened; it became a
promenade; I was able to walk almost without hesitation . . . So
ended the hardest rock climb Bell and I had ever done'. And then
dinner and a bottle of wine:'We fell asleep with our heads on the
table before it was through'. His companion J H B Bell was a
Scottish doctor and a notable climber in his day, and once in a
second-hand bookshop I found a book by Smythe with the author's
dedication to Bell handwritten on the flyleaf. I bought it and have
it now.

The next time I tried rock climbing I didn't mean to. I set off
for a rendezvous in Glen Coe with a doctor friend, Alastair, and a
party of Czech climbers who were visiting Scotland. Communism
in Europe was crumbling and Vaclav Havel had just become
president in Czechoslovakia's first democratic election, so it seemed
newsworthy to talk to them. However, when I arrived at the
Clachaig Inn with my colleague Edna, leader writer on the Herald
and a keen walker, most of the Czechs had already left and Pavel,
the only one remaining, suggested to Alastair that they should try an
easy climb together. A small voice which I recognised as my own
piped up:'Can I come too?'

Alastair said it would be all right, and I reckoned he'd
know. As a doctor, he'd spent several years researching mountain
accidents. Lanky, black-haired Alastair had climbed in the Tatra
mountains of Czechoslovakia the year before and had organised this
return visit. Lazily, we sat outside the Clachaig and sipped coffee,
quizzing Pavel about politics back home. He was delighted with the
election result. He'd been to the West seven years earlier and on his
return was stopped at customs and accused of spying because he'd
brought back a computer for the Prague scientific institute where

he worked. From then on he'd been officially considered unsound.

The party split into walkers and climbers and we climbers set off briskly, six of us heading for Aonach Dubh. Someone had lent me a harness and climbing boots several sizes too small which clenched my toes horribly. I took my last serene look at the scenery from the top of a rock with a budding rowan tree sprouting from it. The burn sped downwards in its gorge and far below tiny cars parked in the laybys sparkled in the sunshine. I munched a sandwich and brooded on the imminent ascent.

I roped up between the muscular Martin, who was trousered in stripey red and white Uncle Sam pants, and Pavel, shod in football boots with the front studs removed — specialist climbing gear being difficult to get in Czechoslovakia. We surveyed Curving Crack, a disturbing prospect to novice eyes, with big jagged clefts wet and dark with dripping water. Aonach Dubh was thronged. At least three parties were already at work in the neighbourhood and voices boomed around. I watched Martin's stripey backside ascend and in due course I was called to scrabble my way after him to the safety of a grassy ledge on which was a stunted tree to which I clung lovingly while waiting my turn on the second pitch. That accomplished, we progressed to a climb called Twilight Arête. Martin led again and I watched apprehensively as he approached a tricky projecting corner. He stretched athletically round the angle and disappeared. I tried to follow but stuck at the corner.

'Reach for the big foothold', Martin shouted from above. 'Feel for it'.

I reached, felt for it, found it with my left foot. I snaked my left hand round the corner and crooked my fingers in a cranny. But what next? I was suspended, spreadeagled, with my right foot locked on the wrong side, a big drop below and no guts to launch myself into space. So I pulled back and descended to solid ground, making way for Pavel, whose nimble footwork I admired as he tiptoed round the awkward corner with scarce a pause for thought.

Subdued, I waited till Alastair appeared with husband and wife team Sam and Carolyn. I roped up behind them and then

Alastair led us to what he gleefully pronounced 'an absolute classic' named Archer Ridge Direct. I reserved judgment. While they headed upwards one after the other I idly watched two other climbers worming their way round a big overhanging cube of rock and felt sick in the pit of my stomach when one came off and dangled on the rope, gently swaying until he scrabbled a foothold again and could continue.

Now it was my turn. Three heads peered down at me as I worked my way towards the ledge on which they were ensconced. I arrived to find not the comfortably flat shelf that I'd hoped for but a narrow, steeply raked wrinkle on which they stood in ascending order. I had a very good eye-level view of Sam's knee. I noticed particularly his boot, an old walking boot whose upper was parting from the sole. It was somewhere on this ascent that Carolyn announced to Alastair that she was four months' pregnant, which caused him some qualms.

I watched them depart in turn, vanishing behind a bulge. The sun also disappeared and it grew cold in the shade and strangely silent after the bustle of the previous hours. My right knee began to quiver uncontrollably, either through chill, tension, fright or a combination of all three. I tried to relax it by taking the weight off my cramped toes, but there was no room to wriggle. From the corner of my eye I sensed that there were spectacular views but I avoided looking, preferring to study the rock formation and plant life in my immediate surroundings, which I got to know intimately. A few stolen glances across the glen revealed the fissured flank of Am Bodach etched by the rays of the declining sun.

At last the slack rope snaked upwards and I heard the fateful summons. I was soon in difficulty and without warning I was off the rock, suspended in mid air. It was not an unpleasant sensation. Relaxed and comfortable on my swing, I was reluctant to face the rock again. But it had to be done. I was conscious of Martin, who had moved round to see where I was, shouting instructions I couldn't understand. Then I took myself in hand. Get on with it, I scolded myself, and I did. How I got to the top I don't know but I remember my last desperate lunge on to the crest and the welcoming hands that grabbed me. All of us, including me, had big grins on our faces. I believe they were as relieved as I was.

The two groups rejoined at the Clachaig and I stayed late with Edna talking to Pavel. It was long after midnight when I got home. My bedtime book at the time was Eric Newby's A Short Walk in the Hindu Kush and I'd reached the chapter in which he and his companion make their unsuccessful bid on Mir Samir ('The descent was terrible . . . If anything happened to one of us it would be the end for both'). All night long my sleep was broken by visions of dizzying cliffs to which I clung by my fingertips, ever on the point of dropping into the abyss.

Mary and I booked a climbing course at Glenmore Lodge, the outdoors centre near Aviemore. I had broken my ankle two months before the start of the course so I had eight weeks to get fit. I persuaded a reluctant doctor to cut off the plaster early and consulted Scottish Ballet's physiotherapist, exercised like mad and went swimming daily. I hobbled round Edinburgh with a stick covering the festival and every morning at seven I went for a workout in the health centre in the basement of my Edinburgh hotel.

The climbing course lasted a week and every day bar one the weather was foul. Raging winds and bitter temperatures kept us off the Cairngorms and confined us to less exposed lower crags. The one bright exception was an outing to the seaside when we hauled ourselves up yellow sandstone cliffs at Cummingstown on the Moray Firth, while the sun shone and the incoming tide lapped at the rock pillars. Even on that relatively calm day there were white horses in the bay. Far out on the blue sea an oil platform lay at anchor.

Glenmore Lodge was built in the fifties and looked very much of its time (though it has been modernised since); a timber building with big windows and flat roofs and spartan accommodation. Mary and I were fortunate to be allocated a tiny bunkroom to ourselves at the end of a corridor.

Each morning after breakfast we collected our gear, the ropes, harness, slings, hard hats, clips, wedges and other ironmongery and piled into a minibus for the drive to the day's chosen obstacle course. There we split into pairs, each couple with an instructor. We started on crags above Kingussie where soldiers were already training on the rock, young lads in denims being harried up and down by barking sergeants. Mary, who soon showed a flair for climbing – she was much better than I – was fascinated by our instructor, Libby, who was young, friendly and wonderfully adept on rock.

'She's just like a cat', Mary whispered to me as we watched her progress above us. Secretly Mary hoped to emulate her.

One morning we woke to see the Cairngorm summits dusted with the first snow of the season. Chilled fingers were in prospect. The wind was blasting and the minibus team showed a marked reluctance to get to grips with granite. On the way we stopped at a tea room, all chintzy prim with tablecloths and bone china, and scoffed hot buttered scones and jam in a ruffianly babel that must have dismayed the regular customers. Our destination was a wooded gorge where the rock rises from the bed of a small river. At the start I tore my hand, and the couple who followed grumbled at finding little puddles of blood in some of the hand holds.

The weather was at its worst on our final day. The group split up and Libby took us to crags near a remote lochan. It was already spitting with rain when we left her car and all morning we were chilled by lashing squalls. We munched our lunch glumly.

The last pitch led over a jutting chunk of rock to a small ledge from which stuck a stubborn little shrub. I was on the end of the rope and as I worked my way over the projecting rock I looked up to see two small white faces peering down at me from beside the shrub.

'Ready when you are', came the familiar call to climb.

'Climbing', I replied – the usual formula.

The rock streamed with near freezing water, the wind whistled round my ears and I swore. The watchers in the gallery heard this and took note. There was a pause, and silently we arrived at an instant consensus. The two shivering women indicated that if I had no burning ambition to join them they wouldn't insist on it. Without more ado the climb was abandoned. Abseiling down, I landed in a jaggy briar bush, the final indignity. Hot chocolate with a large measure of rum in it at a cafe in Aviemore restored the circulation.

Mary missed the farewell do at the Winking Owl (an Aviemore pub) that night. She was unwell – it seemed she'd caught a chill – and I left her in her bunk clutching a hot water bottle. When I got back she was asleep.

Mary loved being in the hills more than anyone I know, and the freedom and joy she found there was infectious. In the hills she could forget care and the pressures of her daily life.

She was in form on An Caisteal (one of the Crianlarich hills): I see her small figure stepping out ahead of me along Twistin Ridge in the teeth of a bitter northerly. We sheltered below the summit for the briefest of halts before retreating from the exposed ridge down a squashy slope to the tractor track that follows the Falloch river in its glen. Mary diverged and had to pass through a herd of tousled cattle grazing with their calves, which slightly unnerved her – a feeling I recognise. I'm wary of all animals including farm beasts. 'Man butted to death by goat' is a headline I remember.

We proposed yet another attempt on the elusive Ben Oss. After a spell of torrential rains a better day was forecast and sure enough, on the way north shafts of sunlight dappled the hills and ragged cloud raced across opening patches of blue. But by the time we parked in the usual spot near Dalrigh farm between Crianlarich and Tyndrum the rain was battering on the windscreen. We were reluctant to leave the car and sipped hot coffee which steamed up the windows. But there was no escape; we struggled into waterproofs and ventured out. Trusting the forecast, I didn't wear overtrousers and paid for it by getting so wet that the rainwater eventually flushed from sodden pants straight into my boots.

Our plan was to approach the hill via the sheltered corrie rather than by tackling it directly over the steep northern ridge, on which we would have felt the force of a near gale. We crossed the Cononish river and the railway and found a faint track through a boggy field to a plank bridge over the Cononish tributary burn. Four Burberried fishermen were tracking the spate downstream, hoping for sport. The path winds through an open birch and pinewood, always upwards, and over exposed tree roots now wet and slippery. The ground was spongey and the tawny carpet of fallen leaves and needles often degenerated into a slushing soup of black peat. Little rivulets churned through the undergrowth on all sides. We walked for a while alongside the main stream as it tumbled over small falls, parting company with it where it came dashing over a deep slabby drop in a fan of spouting channels.

Two high stiles took us out of the forest and then the path petered out, leaving us to tramp over rough heather and coarse grass in a lumpy landscape seamed with a network of soggy channels. We decided on the spot not to return by the same tedious route. Either one of the two ridges enclosing the corrie offered a practical alternative, the one on our left, with its craggy slopes and humpy back, appearing the more challenging and therefore more alluring.

The gale hit us as we approached the crest of the headwall. A little further on, the lochan lying between Oss and Dubhchraig lay grey and unwelcoming. Our intended route was on our right, leading sharply down a turmoil of rocks to a bealach and then steadily upwards to the summit a mile away, heading always straight into the wind.

On the other hand . . .

Only a quarter of a mile away in the other direction Dubhchraig raised its pointy peak. The choice was not difficult. We turned our back on Oss again and set off in the opposite direction – the wind at our backs – staggering now and then, with our jackets whipping round buttocks and thighs. Traversing just below the top of the ridge to escape the worst of the storm, we emerged clutching hands for safety, heading towards the summit cairn topped by a skew-whiff baton of rock. A quick look around over cloud-swept summits (Ben Lui shrouded as usual) and tawny southern flat lands glinting with pools, lochans and watercourses, sufficed.

The ridge descends in a series of step-like crags, and at the first sheltered spot we sat down sat with our backs against a cold rock, commanding the whole length of Loch Lomond, sun-streaked under a warning sky, with the blue outline of the Arran peaks showing on the horizon.

It was a mistake to go into the plantation (it nearly always is), but we were seduced by the sight of a forest road on the far side of the glen which we knew would take us back to Dalrigh. It's true there was a burn to cross but there was a wooden bridge in view. A swathe of young spruce trees separated us from the burn, but since it was a recent planting and the growth was spindly and immature there seemed little to impede us. Too late, we discovered that they grew on broken ground trenched by swift burns and deep drains, and moreover, slabs of maturer forest intervened. A couple of high deer fences also barred the way, though we found a rough and ready gateway where someone had cut the wires and looped them back, and elsewhere a section had been flattened, allowing access. We were happy to benefit by vandalism, if vandalism it was (I consider it equally reprehensible to bar the way to the hills by planting impenetrable thickets of conifer). It was a relief to gain the forest road.

The army was abseiling in Glen Croe as we made for Beinn an Lochain; men in green fatigues strung out on the tumbling outcrops below the Cobbler. From the top of the Rest and Be Thankful we walked past Loch Restil till we could jump the stream.

A fine ridge leads like a ramp to Beinn an Lochain's summit, give or take the odd twist and bump and an abrupt lurch upwards some way short of the top. A short marshy wallow followed by a twist or two on a grassy slope brought us on to this ridge where we located a faint path, not much more than a strip of flattened vegetation with footholes cut into the steeper inclines. Since Beinn an Lochain isn't a Munro (it was once – it's yet another dislodged from the list by later calculations), the baggers hadn't yet beaten a trail on it. Here and there it was steep enough for us to put out a hand, and occasionally we had to search for sure footholds on wet shelves of rock.

Near the big lurch we stopped to talk to a couple of veteran walkers and survey the way ahead. We could identify a route winding up the rocky front and just above it, a rack of tilted rock forming a saw-edged crest. The top was lost in cloud. As we advanced we were pushed about by a strong south-easterly, dauntingly at a narrow corner not much wider than the path, with steep drops on either side. A few weeks after our expedition a woman died on the Beinn when snow was about – was it at that point that she slipped and fell? The cairn came into view sooner than expected and we didn't stop, not wanting to make a crowd – a group of people were already huddled there eating their lunch.

We picked an escape route down a steep chimney between crags, clambering down on a mixture of loose stone and wet grass. Once on the open hill – grass mingled with reeds – we spotted our car, a small white speck far below which we kept in sight from then on. Other cars tightly parked around the head of Loch Long indicated a rush on the Cobbler and its companion hills, and the A83 over the Rest was buzzing with traffic en route to Inveraray, including a noisy column of bikers.

Since it was still early in the afternoon we made a detour for refreshment, but the miles across moorland to the village of Lochgoilhead proved fruitless. At Herb's Bar on the waterfront ('Good Food, Unusual Wines') a printed notice told us that 'owing to Scotland's antiquated licensing laws we must stop serving at 2.30 on Sundays'. As we stood reading the notice, a man – was it Herb himself? – came out and locked the door behind him. It wasn't Herb of course; there is no such person. On a later visit I saw that the restaurant above the pub was called the Bouquet Garni. Herb's Bar was a pun.

Beinn an Lochain is quite testing and Mary, eager to try out her new crampons, was already looking forward to a return visit in winter. But it was her last hill.

I returned one evening from a solo walk a fortnight later and phoned to tell her about it. No one answered.

Later my phone rang. I could barely recognise the small voice, painfully hoarse and feeble. She was calling from hospital.

Recently she'd had bouts of unexplained sickness, and for the past few days she'd been unwell and depressed, but hadn't seen a doctor. Now she was telling me there had been an emergency. There would be tests in the morning and she didn't think I'd be able to visit.

'I'll be at the hospital', I said. 'Try to sleep'.

I went to bed troubled.

It was graver than she or I could guess. There was internal bleeding and complications set in that overwhelmed her slight body. She struggled through the night but in the morning she slipped away. She died at eight o'clock on the last day of October.

A month later, on a day of sparkling frost and clear blue sky, I scattered her ashes on a mountain top in Glen Coe, with the snowy peaks around her.

Part Two

O*THER*
*l*ands

10
Ghosts of war

I once spent three consecutive Septembers walking trail routes (or *randonnées*) in France. It was before I'd met Mary and my partner on those expeditions was Edith – tall, dark-haired, a keen musician and a great travelling companion who never let herself be stumped by a foreign language when she needed to communicate with the locals. She smiled appealingly, dredged up the shreds of her school French, and when that failed achieved wonders with speaking gestures.

We struck an autumn heatwave in the Vosges mountains of Alsace. One morning as the sun grew hot we decided to have a gentle stroll in the forest before pressing on. We zigzagged down through woods to the blue circle of the Lac du Ballon where a couple on the shore had steaks sizzling on a barbecue and a bottle of Bordeau uncorked. Among the trees a woodcutter was at work, the clunk reaching our ears a split second after each stroke of the axe. Then in the afternoon we ambled along a narrow track over hillsides where blaeberries grew, picking them for dessert. As I stooped for a last handful of the fruit I glanced back the way we'd just come. The blue sky was seeded with puffy clouds but in the distance above the horizon lay a strange cloud-like layer, white in colour, flat and shimmering below but spiked and battlemented on top. As I looked, this vision resolved itself into the snowy peaks of the Alps more than a hundred miles to the south, rising like the towers of a distant city, a long Manhattan of icy skyscrapers. It was a dreamscape.

Our destination that night was an out of season ski resort, a settlement spread out over a high plateau like a town in the old West. This impression was heightened by the approach of a cantering black horse with a man on its back dressed in cowboy hat and high-heeled boots (and maybe spurs, though I didn't notice). He clattered past, put the lumbering horse over a low jump and disappeared round the corner of a bar. No doubt he hitched his horse to the rail and burst through swing doors, ka-doing, ka-doing, Western style, though I can't swear to it.

We took an upstairs room in the neighbouring Hotel Belle-Vue, which justified its name, for the views were panoramic. Later we dined with the Alps in sight again, and watched them fade at last into the pink and blue haze of dusk.

In the morning I walked out early leaving Edith asleep, up a grassy slope to the top of a hill called the Jungfrauenkopf, which was sadly cluttered with ski-lift cantilevers and hawsers. Looking southwards, I saw the Alps again. Peaks floated like islands on the morning haze, and below them the nearer hills unfolded in a sea of blue waves. The peaks seemed to be half way up the sky and I had to raise my eyes to see them. One, I felt sure, was the Matterhorn; there could be no mistaking that slender, crooked pyramid – but I was wrong. Later in the hotel dining room I studied a panoramic photograph and my supposed Matterhorn proved to be the Finsterarhorn, with the Streckhorn and the caliper crest of the Wetterhorn beside it. That was the last I saw of the Alps. Though we wandered the crests of Alsace for a fortnight more, they never swam into view again.

The Vosges form a dramatic barrier on France's eastern flank. They are green hills, rising steeply to modest peaks, with the occasional outcrop of rock, and their lower slopes are often heavily forested. Here and there small blue lochans lie in the valley floors. Sometimes you find a castle on a summit, though we were more interested in the small auberges which are spaced at decent intervals along the way. This is wine country. Vineyards terrace the eastern slopes and the villages below are familiar points on the wine route.

A guidebook describes it as 'an area almost Alpine in character (though not in elevation), with glacial moraines, meadows, narrow valleys and cliffs'. It was a tempting invitation –

how could we resist? We packed our bags and went.

The first days were misty and we even had rain, mostly one night when lightning flickered and thunder rolled, drowning the faint clangour of cowbells in the surrounding fields. The next morning I found the little girl of the house nose to nose at the window with a cow on the other side. In the dank air the beast puffed billows of steam from its nostrils while the child chortled with delight.

The scenery was pleasantly mixed. There were steep and sometimes rugged ascents to many of the peaks, alternating with stretches of level or gently undulating country. Sometimes we'd be canopied in a tunnel of green foliage, at others we'd be on open heath where the dry ground gave out a hollow ring with every step. There were purple heather slopes and stretches of jarring boulders or rough pavements of pink granite slabs. On the day of our longest walk when the guidebook failed us (it omitted a significant section of of the route, which added three hours to our day) we passed through clearings of felled woodland where resinous pine scented the air. Mostly we walked on footpaths which, though they often seemed remote, were never far from the roadway and often crossed it. This highway, which parallels the wine route on the valley floors, was engineered to give access for men and munitions in war and it follows, more or less, the line of the crests, often climbing by tortuous hairpins to the high passes between the summits. Now it is used by tourists. Bus parties drive up to some of the most impressive outlooks and we might emerge at the top, grubby after a hard day's walking in lonely country, to find a roadside staging post swarming with chattering trippers in high heels and sunhats.

Everywhere we went we were haunted by grim reminders of war, sometimes in the most peaceful and lonely places. No one was about at the Camp Turenne. This was a meeting of the ways, broad tracks metalled with rough stone to allow wheeled vehicles passage, and now overgrown. We met no one all day but a man in white shorts and singlet with a pack on his back, loping down a steep slope. The sun was fierce and we were glad of the patchy shelter offered by the forest. At frequent openings in the trees we looked down on the plain below. The Camp Turenne, silent and deserted now, had once resounded to the noise of marching battalions and the rumble of heavy transport, and the hills around to the blast of guns and the crack of rifle fire.

The first intimation of war had come two days before, near the top of the Ballon d'Alsace. Searching for the auberge on a hilltop shrouded in mist, picking our way between grazing cattle, we came on a white stone sculpture, a naked figure outstretched against the sky, a memorial to the men who tunnelled beneath the lines to blow up enemy positions. Sometimes they broke in on their German counterparts and engaged in hand-to-hand fighting underground, or were blown up themselves by a mine laid by the enemy. Could that be why the stone figure was spreadeagled in the air?

A few days later, as we climbed to the top of the Grand Ballon, the highest peak in the Vosges, we found another memorial, this time the statue of a French soldier in marching order, facing across the Rhine to the Black Forest, enemy territory. The bronze figure, larger than life, was kitted out in a greatcoat with a pack and bedroll on his back and a rifle with fixed bayonet in his hand. His legs were swathed in puttees and the beret on his head bore the hunting horn badge of the Diables Bleu, the blue devils, the famous Chasseurs of the mountains. The blue devils fought a desperate campaign in these beautiful mountains throughout the Great War. Not far away is the site of one of the great battles of that conflict, Vieil Armand in French and Hartmannswillerkopf in German, where 30,000 fell.

To me, the most poignant image of the Great War has always been the muddy wasteland of Belgium and northern France. I hadn't realised that the line of entrenchments stretched the whole length of France to the border with Switzerland, and that the green mountains of the Vosges had been as bitterly contested as Flanders fields. All along these lovely hills battles had been waged. In the snow of winter, in summer sunshine such as we enjoyed, men had struggled up these hills and through this forest, tired, bored, frightened, laden with packs as heavy as ours, and here they had fought and died.

One day we lunched simply in the open air at a roadside inn at a place called Calvaire. We drank cold white wine from glasses beaded with condensation. A little further on we came to a small enclosure in the trees. The squeaky iron gate was embossed with the horn of the Chasseurs Alpins. It was a cemetery, shaded by tall pine trees which must have been planted seventy years before when the earth on the graves was still fresh. A thick layer of brown needles softened the paths between the graves, and cones were scattered where they fell. Sunlight streamed through the foliage.

Edith and I walked among the parterres in silence, not trusting ourselves to speak. We read the names; young men, *morts pour la France*, most of them killed in 1914 and 1915, the first years of the war. Some were nameless. On one grave was a bunch of fresh flowers. Who had put them there? It couldn't have been a widow, and even a son or daughter, elderly now, would have been too young to remember the dead man clearly. Who grieved or felt what pang after so many years?

This graveyard garden seemed infinitely more touching than the white ordered stones in their thousands in the grander war cemeteries. Here the simplicity of a few crosses under the trees was heart-rending.

Some hours later, near the close of the day, after ascending a narrow granite path, we reached the hilltop called La Tête des Faux, and found a fortress in decay. Near this spot, it was written in the guidebook, were fought some of the fiercest encounters of the war. Even in its ruinous state, elaborate fortifications designed to withstand the shock of modern artillery could be traced among the blaeberry bushes and the scrub of stunted pines and other vegetation that threatened to engulf them. Deep trenches walled with masonry gave access to a central bombproof still partly roofed with thick concrete, from which twisted steel girders poked. Dark, narrow winding ways leading to occasional hideouts laced the hillside. On a crest, further fortifications were topped by ramparts formed by sandbag-shaped cement bricks from which the sacking had long since rotted away. Steel shutters still rasped on their hinges or creaked back to reveal slits for rifles.

Men once shuffled along these sunken corridors or stood on guard at their posts, peering at a world gone mad. Looped around these emplacements and tangled far down the hillside were coils of old barbed wire, rusted to a rich golden red. Some of it was piled in twisted heaps in ditches, torn up after the war and left where it lay. For how many men had these entanglements been the final indignity, the last barrier of pain?

It was dusk. The village of Le Bonhomme, a small place on the river below the Tête which had been devastated in the second war, was unwelcoming at first. In a noisy, crowded bar the proprietor looked up from pouring a drink to grunt that there were no rooms. In the street I spoke to a woman brushing the pavement outside a small hotel. She was apologetic. They were closed. In fact, they were going on holiday themselves the next day.

'Wait a moment', she said, 'I'll ask my husband'. And she slipped indoors.

When she came back she was smiling. They would open up for us.

We had a comfortable room. We showered in steaming water. We ate well and drank Rosé d'Alsace with the trout. When we spoke about what we'd seen, the patronne said that her mother, when a little girl in the Great War, had lain in bed listening to the faint cries of a German soldier lying wounded on the hill. 'Mutter, Mutter', she'd heard. A young man in agony, calling for his mother.

We walked along high heathland on the edge of a scarp that dropped sharply towards the Rhine. Every kilometre was marked by a granite stob sunk into the ground, defining the old frontier imposed after Prussia thrashed France in the campaign of 1870-71. On the west side, the letter F had been incised. The equivalent marks on the east were usually obliterated, but the letter D for Deutschland could still be traced on some stones. Most of the Ds must have been chiselled out by patriots, but I never learned whether this had been done during or after the period of annexation.

Wherever we went in this countryside were reminders of its disputed past and evidence of a schizoid inheritance. Two old men we talked to as they drank wine in a cafe at Kayserberg spoke a heavily accented French. Their native tongue, they said, was German but their children had grown up speaking French. A wall plaque in the village marked the birthplace of the French missionary and theologian Albert Schweitzer, born in 1875 and therefore officially German by a margin of four years. When we arrived in the hill village of Mittlach our first stop was at a cafe where the proprietor, a spry old woman in a print frock, drew up a chair and quizzed us in German. *'Wir sind alle zufrieden hier'* (we're all happy here), she said. And she chattered to two young women passing with their babies in a curious patois that seemed to mix both languages.

Place names that look and sound German mingle with French. In the forest we came to successive clearings named on the map Kaesmarkt (which translate as cheese market, a curious idea considering its location) and Teufelsloch, the devil's hole. In the neighbourhood of Aubure is a Rocher du Koenigsstuhl. The Lac Vert and the Lac des Perches are matched by the Lac du Fischboedle and the Lac du Schiessrothried. At the foot of the Vosges on the edge of the Rhine plain cluster villages and small towns, places where gabled, red-tiled, half-timbered houses overhang twisting lanes, whose names evoke the centuries-old cultural tug of war: Guebwiller, Turckheim, Ammerschwihr, Kaysersberg, Mittelwihr, Riquewihr, Chatenois, Ribeauville.

These are familiar halts on the tourist wine route where you can drink the wines of the region at source in numerous caveaux. We started on the booze before the walk. We took a bus from Colmar to Kaysersberg on a savagely hot afternoon and sat in a cool

cavern sipping in succession (tasting, not drinking!) a
gewürtstraminer, two rieslings, tokay, muscadet and pinot noir, the
grand Alsatian quintet.

One of the pleasures of walking these hills is to emerge from
woods or clamber down a steep slope to find a roadside inn with
log benches set out on the verandah and check cloths spread on the
tables inside. If our luck was out we'd turn up to find the auberge
closed for its rest day, usually on a Monday or Tuesday, a great
disappointment. Never closed on a Sunday, of course. I used to scan
the map in the evening trying to identify inns on the following
day's route. One thirsty day we spent more than nine hours on the
trail, far from habitation and with not a hospitable place of
refreshment to be found from start to finish. Bottle water to wash
down hunks of bread and cheese was all we had.

We ate simply. For instance, a bowl of potage and fresh trout
from the Lac des Perches at the Rouge Gazon, a plain place in a
high meadow that looked like a farmhouse. 'Tonight we have
choucroute', said the lady at a small hotel in the village of
Thannenkirch where we slept in a room called Rosalie.
Choucroute is the Alsatian version of sauerkraut, a vinegary dish
neither of us fancied. But when the choucroute came in on an
ashet we discovered it to be a mound of lightly spiced cabbage in
which were nuggets of sausage (two varieties), ham and potato, and
it was delicious.

On the other hand we ate unappetizingly at the Col de la
Schlucht, a viewpoint on the Route des Crêtes where there was no
room at a cosy-looking chalet called the Hotel des Randonneurs (it
was filled by a party of German hikers in woolly hats and
lederhosen). We took a room in a hotel where the price of
accommodation was geared to the grade of evening meal you chose
or vice-versa. Bypassing the *menu gastronomique*, we settled for
bottom of the range and got packet soup and chicken in brown
sauce with flaccid noodles. The patron came to the table in a
tracksuit and asked if we'd enjoyed it and Edith told him straight.

At the other extreme, we dined with a Canadian couple at

the best restaurant in the town of Ribeauville, where there was
starched linen on the table and crystal to drink from. We
rummaged in our rucksacks for clean clothes and tried not to look
like scarecrows.

Brief meetings with interesting people are part of the
attractions of a long-distance walk. We exchanged addresses with
the Canadians, Stewart and Mary, but inevitably, apart from a
Christmas card, I've not kept in touch. David was a young
Australian on sabbatical from work in Sydney. He'd bought an old
Volkswagen in London and was driving round Europe. We were
sitting on a grassy bank when he spoke to us in ropey French and
we answered in the same. The conversation was halting until we
discovered we could all speak English. In David's company we met
Hans and Trussche from Rotterdam.

As we sat by the dark water of the Lac du Fischboedle, Horst
and Gisela from Dusseldorf asked us to take their photograph.
Together we climbed to a mountain inn where Horst and Gisela
announced it was their twenty-second wedding anniversary. I went
to the bar and asked for the best in the cellar, a red wine *cuvée à la
ferme*. We had a jolly time looking over meadows across to distant
hills while a tribe of black and gold hens clucked and pecked
around us.

The walk was nearly over. After almost three weeks of Indian
summer the weather became autumnal. We set off in early morning
crispness, our boots wet in the dew-laden grass. The trees were
marked with browns and yellows. Rainbows formed in the spray of
a cascade that tumbled over a rocky cliff edge.

It was our longest day. There were many miles to cover and
we lost our way more than once. Towards evening we traversed an
overgrown path on the edge of a ravine whose slopes recently had
been cleared of forest, leaving a sad brash of broken branches
among the stumps. We were tired and bad tempered. Tangles of
low growth, thorns and roots impeded our way and scratched our
bare legs, and we often stumbled. As we reached better ground and

the way ahead became clearer, we rounded a small hill and in the slanting light of the setting sun saw a thin foil of honey-coloured stone outlined against the sky. When we reached it we found that a larger than life figure of a man was cut in shallow relief on the inner curve. It was a monument to victims of the Nazis.

This was the site of a forced labour camp near the village of Natzweiler. Here 30,000 Jews and political prisoners died during the war. Many succumbed to famine and exhaustion as they struggled up the steep route from the valley laden with building materials. First they were forced to hack out wide terraces on the hillside and then to build the barrack huts in which they were to live. Captured resistance fighters were shot there, and during the later years of the war a ghoulish anatomical museum at Strasbourg displayed the skeletons of a number of Jews murdered at the camp.

The wooden huts, menacingly neat and orderly, are preserved as a museum, but it was closed when we found it. The barbed wire perimeter fence was still in place and over the rough timber arch of the gateway was the evilly ironic motto *Arbeit macht frei*. Death was the only liberation for many. Edith went into the camp and walked around outside the huts but I couldn't follow. I'd no stomach for it. I sat on a stone above the camp as the sun set.

Last day. It was to have been the Donon, the most northerly height of the Vosges. By then we would have traversed the whole range from south to north, reaching the top of every considerable hill on the way.

This day we would walk light, leaving most of our gear at the station in the town of Schirmek. The station was ominously quiet. Nothing moved on the lines as we crossed the bridge. At the ticket office we were told there was a strike, which caused us some anxiety as we had to leave that evening for Strasbourg. But it was a half-hearted strike. The man at the desk assured us the trains would be running by six.

It became hot again. We walked in the shade of a beech coppice until we emerged at a bend in the roadway where there was a small hotel. Inside, a group of jolly Germans were gulping jugs of beer. We sat on the terrace and ordered two glasses of wine, and then two more. The heat warmed our brown flesh pleasantly and we felt no urgent need to press on.

There was said to be a fine panoramic view from the top of the Donon, but it was a view we never saw. We sat indolently for a while, and when we moved it was lazily in the other direction. We returned to Schirmek by road, passing an old disused foundry with a handsome brick chimney stalk, and the end of a valley leading to a village called Les Miniêres (a centre of the rural iron industry in days gone by). We had tea in a prim tearoom, and at six precisely the strikers returned and took us away.

In the next two autumns Edith and I followed the line of France's eastern hills down through the Jura into Switzerland. Then there was a gap of some years, and when I returned to walk in France I went to the Midi, in the south, and on my own.

11

The Orient Express stops here

It was noon and the Provençal sun was hot. The bus ground up the incline in a low gear and pulled up in a small dusty square. The driver got out and strolled off to chat with the locals and I followed, lugging my pack awkwardly down the steps. Across the road was a store with farm machinery and assorted ironmongery. I asked for alcohol.

Alcool. Could that be right? The liquid looked right, it smelt right and it was the word the French-English dictionary gave for meths, so I sat on a sandy bank and poured it into the red flask marked Fuel I'd brought for the purpose. Airlines don't care to transport your inflammables.

Now I had everything. I had a tent, a bivvy bag, a sleeping bag, a stove, and lastly, fuel. I had a new jumbo rucksack that weighed a ton. I also had a hernia, but that could wait till I got home.

St Martin-Vesubie lies high in the foothills of the Maritime Alps, thirty miles or so north of Nice and close to the Italian border. Alastair, the friend who'd hauled me up a rock face in Glen Coe, had suggested St Martin as a starting point. He and friends had spent a fortnight rock climbing in the area and he was enthusiastic. Wonderful country, he said. I'd find plenty of huts in the mountains, like the Cougourde, north of St Martin.

'But watch out for the *gardien* (warden)', he warned. 'He's a dragon'.

The best way to reach the Cougourde is to take a taxi to the hamlet of Le Boréon, which is half a dozen miles as the crow flies from St Martin. Allowing for bends in the road it must be considerably further. But after a flight to Paris, the overnight train to the Midi, the bus run from Nice and a night in a bunk at St Martin, I was itching to take the trail and in no mood to hire transport. It seemed better to walk over the hill to Le Boréon, mostly in forest but with a long stretch in the open leading to a summit where the map promised a viewpoint. It would take 1,300 metres of continuous ascent to reach the Cime de Piagu, but trek-heavy as I was I set off hopefully.

Once out of the forest I could see bare brown rock ahead, but the bright sun of morning had failed, obliterated by threatening blackness and a ring of hammerhead clouds. Forked lightning pierced the gloom and a peal of thunder boomed around the tops. Up there I felt isolated and exposed. The lightning continued to flit and the thunder rolled nearer, or so I imagined. I walked on for a little and then as the first blobs of rain spattered the pale rock at my feet I took stock, reconsidered the options and abandoned the ascent. For the rest of the day it rained steadily and I took a lower route along muddy trails and under dripping foliage while the thunder, after a few crashing chords, gradually receded.

Apart from a solitary angler shrouded in oilskins, thigh deep in brown water and motionless as a statue, no one was about at Le Boréon. A gaily painted signboard showing pine trees and snowy peaks pointed to a gîte further up the hill, somewhere to stay. 'Beds and meal at all seasons', it said. A lie. I found the door padlocked, the windows barred, the place deserted.

But the Hotel du Lac had a welcome for me and trout from the lake for dinner. Sinking into a wicker chair before the TV, I watched football (Red Star Belgrade beat Marseille) and then took myself to bed in a little room at the end of the corridor with beams across the ceiling. Before I drifted off I heard the young couple who ran the hotel make love in the adjoining room, with the tail of their dog drumming an accompaniment on the floor.

The young patron was confident. 'It's going to be fine today', he said.

Wrong. Soon it clouded over and the day remained damp and misty on the higher ground, though there was no more rain and only one thunder clap at 11.30 precisely, as if it struck by the half hour. At first I followed a woody glen where a stream came tumbling down among pine trees, passing a meadow where shiny milk churns stood outside a large stone byre – one of the many *vâcheries* found in the summer pastures.

High up and almost at the treeline, where the stream was no more than a small burn tumbling over stones, I came to a pond with a chalet beside it and stopped for a word with two green-clad rangers (the area is in the Mercantour national park) who gave me bad news about the Cougourde. I could reach it in spite of the snow, they said, but it was shut.

This was a blow. If the Cougourde was shut what chance was there of finding the other huts and refuges open? I'd assumed that late snow might be an obstacle. What I hadn't known was that few of the huts opened until at least the middle of June. And it was only the end of May. I'd have to change my plans.

In the meantime I decided to make a day of it. The first traces of snow occurred here and soon I was making my way over great beds of it, following a track marked by paint splashes on trees and rocks. Latterly these, like everything else on ground level, were hidden by the snow. At regular intervals there had been tall timber signposts numbered in sequence. Near the top of the pass I looked in vain for post No. 427 until I spotted a mere six inches of it poking through. All but the top of the nine-foot post was buried in snow.

I dumped my rucksack on a boulder, grasped my ice axe and kicked a way up to the pass. Once there I looked into a wide amphitheatre, a flat snowy expanse hemmed in by misty heights of bare rock and snowy gullies, with here and there a few clumps of ragged conifers on the slopes. It was old snow, blotched and streaked brown with swathes of dead vegetation, mainly pine needles, which the winds of several months had swept over the surface.

Invisible under a carpeting of snow and ice and discernible only by a flatness in the surface lay the Lac de Trecolpas, the lake which should have been the pearl of the scene. It was not inviting. If I'd been made of sterner mettle I'd have set up camp. I had the equipment, but not the will.

I clumped back down the snowy bank, shouldered my sack and came down to the treeline again on a bouldery track that often became the bed of a running stream. An alternative track that passed a grand spuming waterfall took me to the bottom.

As I passed the car park in the trees I saw three familiar figures, a spry elderly couple and a younger women whom I'd met in the morning as they prepared to set out on a different route. Tea at the hotel? I climbed into their car and we sped down to Le Boréon for hot chocolate and teacakes. They offered a lift back to St Martin which I gratefully accepted. It would have been a wearisome walk.

I shared the gîte at St Martin with a jolly party of ten from Toulon led by Jean-Luc, a tall, rangy man with hair cascading over his shoulders, who was training to join the elite band of professional Alpine guides. Three of his group were municipal gardeners, another a teacher who insisted on airing her English – which was as duff as my French.

They had their own quarters in the gîte, and two other men slept in the small room where I found a billet. This pair were more or less resident. They came from Chamonix and were climbers, but spent much of the year working on the roads, fixing wire netting over cliff-like cuttings to prevent rockfall, a job that exercised their climbing skills. In high summer they quit the roads for the mountains where they dug out crystals from inaccessible places to sell to collectors. For this they used power drills, and I imagined birds put to flight and chamois darting over the screes as they shattered the peace of the lonely places.

It was Hélène, the *gardienne*, who recommended a new route for me, now that my first plan of campaign had been abandoned. She suggested I make for an idyllic spot called Les Granges de la Brasque where there were splendid views, spring water to drink and plenty of opportunity to camp. By heading south-west from Les Granges I could start on a sweep which would eventually bring me back full circle among the mountains. I had more than three weeks in hand. By the time I was back in the mountains the snow would have retreated a little and huts might be open.

Morning found me walking through glades where dewy undergrowth brushed against my legs and the sun shone on the Vesubie valley below me. At a hilltop village (*Non au Parc* painted on the wall, a slogan directed against the creation of the national park, probably by local hunters) I had a lemonade in the bar before tackling the long ascent to a pass called the Col du Varaire, where I met the only person to cross my path on the hills that day, a walker in bright check shorts who came striding down from one of the neighbouring peaks. He gave me a friendly warning as I sat resting on a fallen tree whose mossy bark was a mountain landscape in miniature – all crags and canyons.

'You'll have to be a bit careful up there', he said, pointing to crags above. 'There's snow'.

Sure enough I had to cross snow-filled gullies and since the angles were steep I took out the axe. Then I had a two-mile walk over the bare hillside, keeping always below a line of jagged crests. Once again the weather changed, and on this bleak section I faced showers of hail, sleet and then rain.

It was a day of contrasts, the final transformation coming when I crossed into a region of sandy turf and green pastures cropped by countless sheep. Their pungent droppings were everywhere and I could hear the dull clank of their bells. Suddenly they were all round me, hundreds of them, big, long-legged beasts with close-curled fleece the colour of old sandstone, unlike any breed I know at home. Sheep in penny numbers are silly harmless creatures but to find them milling around me en masse was disconcerting. Something had alarmed them, perhaps my presence, and they came stampeding past at a fast trot, bells jangling and hooves drumming. I stood still in their midst, and where their headlong flight took them I do not know. No shepherd came to gather his flock.

The Granges de la Brasque lay alongside a narrow road that

curved round the valley. It had the air of a deserted village. There were a few small timber huts which might have been holiday chalets – pretty basic if they were – or a school summer camp. No one was about. There was also a derelict stone church, the walls still standing but the roof caved in and the windows gone, and when I pushed open the heavy warped door I found the interior stripped bare and filled with the sharp scent of dung. Animal droppings covered the space where the altar had been. Outside on a patch of level ground were a number of large stones, all carved with emblems – crossed cannon, anchors, or a bugle – and some had dates on them from before the war. It looked like a military camp site from the 1930s.

A quarter of a mile away I found the spring among thin woods. Crystal water flowing from a source on the hillside jetted through spouts into a wooden trough decorated with painted alpine flowers, before dribbling away in many channels through an oozy dell. Beside it a sign warned that *la Nature n'est pas une poubelle. Ramenez vos ordures chez vous* – Nature isn't a dustbin. Take your rubbish home. With great care, therefore, not to disfigure the surroundings, I prepared my first (and as it happened, my last) camp site of the journey. The sun had set when at last, having cooked and eaten my meal, I eased myself down the green tunnel of the tent and fell asleep.

I woke to one of those scenes which, so the converted say, make camping bliss. Birds sang, a cuckoo called, and when I poked my head out I saw the valley all hazy and blue hills outlined on the horizon. Swathes of morning mist lifted from the dark green of the mountainside, thickly wooded from top to bottom. The sun had not yet risen above the hills but the sky was clear.

I was poised for an early start but there was breakfast to be got, water from the spouting stream to be boiled, the tent to strike and my belongings to pack, which as usual took far longer that I thought possible. When I set out on the road it was nearly eleven, the sun had cleared the trees and it was hot already.

The feature of the day was a passage through an arid

limestone ravine under towering cliffs, following a track that led over many scree slopes. Once I lost the path. I was close under a rock face heavily vegetated with shrubs, thorns and stunted trees, and at first the way seemed to lead upwards through all this. I struggled through the underbrush with my pack snagging and threatening to tumble me back down until it became manifestly impossible to progress. From the height I'd gained I could now see where I'd gone wrong. The point where the track took a sharp turn over rubble had been indistinguishable at ground level, but from above it could be seen as a faint thread twisting over blue-white stones. I part scrambled, part slid down the slope, cursing the thorns which ripped flesh and clothes. A short distance ahead I had to edge cautiously round a rock that hung over an abyss, nervous in case some unnoticed protuberance might catch the heavy rucksack and tilt me over.

From then on it was plain sailing down a long slope towards Roquebillière, a small town that fixed itself in my mind, country and western style, as Rockabilly. Rockabilly: I sang it to myself along the way. In the valley bottom by the river (still the Vesubie) an extensive commercial camp site with family tents and caravans drawn up in ranks did not attract the wilderness walker. I crossed by a high ancient bridge void of traffic – that was diverted over a modern bridge – in the centre of which a game of pétanque was being hotly disputed, and I had to stand aside while a boule was cast.

It was five o'clock, getting late, but I pushed on to the next red-roofed village, up on a hilltop and aptly named Belvédère. Enquiries took me to the baker's shop where a lady behind the counter was serving pastries. Could she direct me to the gîte?

Who better? *'Le gîte, c'est moi'*, she said.

Madame la Boulangère summoned her husband to drive me there. Half-way down the hill we turned into a flower-bordered courtyard where the electronic gate opened unbidden, and stopped in front of a large garage. Out bounded a big black dog, barking.

'Down, Diablo', commanded his master and Diablo (an

obedient devil) subsided, flat on his belly like a cur.

We entered the garage. On the far wall was a low door with a creaking grille which led into the gîte. Inside was a room with small lace-curtained windows, a table with a vase of dried flowers on it, and a rack of books and magazines, and beyond that, through another doorway, a dormitory with beds of all sizes including bunks, a double bed and a platform with a mattress on it big enough, by the look of it, to sleep four and a little one side by side. Monsieur le Boulanger said that the previous week ten bikers on a rally had slept there, the maximum. But I had it to myself.

I liked my gîte in a garage so well I stayed for two nights. Next day, Sunday, I made a day of rest. I sat in the church square and watched the village come to life. Men in blue shirts gathered to gossip by a sunny wall and women criss-crossed the square carrying baguettes. The church bell began to clang and suddenly there was a flux of churchgoers and the square filled with chatter.

Once they'd all disappeared inside I strolled over to the public notice board where I read a potted history of the area. It had been part of the kingdom of Sardinia in the eighteenth century, was then briefly integrated with revolutionary France before being handed back on the defeat of Napoleon, and in due course it became (reluctantly) part of unified Italy. It wasn't until the 1947 peace treaty that these disputed mountain villages returned to French rule. The soldiers honoured in the local war memorials died fighting in the western desert for Italy.

I explored the narrow cobbled back streets (one of them called the Rue Obscure), and then wandered beyond the village. A notice in a field said, according to my suspect translation, 'putting worms (maggots?) in the manure is forbidden. Offenders will be prosecuted'. I wondered why anyone should want to put worms in the dung, and even if they did, what harm would it do?

In the evening I sat and read old copies of Paris Match from the bookshelf. There were pictures of flooding in Nîme, with brown water surging down the main street and a school bus full of children floating away. There was a story of a busy week on Everest when Marc Batard, *le Sprinter du Toit du Monde*, climbed it in a record 22 hours, Jean-Marc Boivin paraglided from the top, and journalist Michel Parmentier was lost in an avalanche near the summit. And there was the adventure of the Pope in the Dolomites. A picture showed the white-haired old man pausing for breath on a narrow ledge. He was roped to a trinity of guides, two men and a woman, who were carrying all the gear while Jean-Paul walked light in flat cap, shirt and baggy trousers. Once at the top of the 2,600-metre Peralba he dropped to his knees before the statue of the virgin and child and gave thanks for the ascent.

I was on the road again a little before eight in the morning. Madame la Boulangère in a negligée popped her head out of an upstairs window, waved and shouted, *'Bonne journée'*, and even Diablo managed a perfunctory wag of the tail. Down wet and weedy paths I went, up to another hilltop village called La Bollène, then down again by a stream rushing madly along a concrete chute. Where did all the water come from in this dry limestone countryside? Even Belvédère on its peak rang with the sound of running waters. There must have been a multitude of springs.

Another ascent, and a long one, took me from the Vesubie valley bottom to the shoulder of the Cime de l'Escaletta, a hill called Staircase. There was no respite from the zigzags. Now I would be facing north, glimpsing through breaks in the trees the distant rooftops of La Bollène and Belvédère clustered on their eminences, now southwards over rolling green hills towards the plain of maritime Provence. I set a steady pace and kept at it without pause. In all, I climbed about 1,400 feet in an hour, which is good going when heavily laden, on steep ground, in broiling midday heat. It was best that way. Anything else would have been slow torture.

I was helped by my stick. Most days I'd pick up a stick from the forest and it marvellously eased the pain on long ascents. Once a good rhythm had been established there was pleasure in the steady swing and stab of the staff. Climbing Staircase Hill I found a measure of four steps to one swing of the stick served for the lesser gradients, reducing to three steps or even two on steeper ground. I became a connoisseur of walking sticks. The trick was to find one reasonably straight and free of snags, with smooth bark for a comfortable grip. I could whittle away awkward jags with my penknife. I took an aesthetic pleasure in these sticks – one, species of origin unknown, had an attractive reddish tint in the bark. A stick has a springy feel in the hand and it rings out pleasantly with a variety of tones on hard ground and stony tracks. One day, walking through open sunlit woods on a downhill stretch from the snowy mountains I had a clean, straight, tapering hazel stick with a kink worn smooth near the top, just fine for the the hand to clasp, and it was a stick to sing to. I carried a telescopic ski pole strapped to my pack which was useful in snow but no match on dry ground for a staff cut from the tree. Your stick has a soul, not like plastic.

The fine morning deteriorated. When I reached a broad track bulldozed through the forest a steady downpour began. I had to break a way through the dripping undergrowth where felling operations enforced a detour through a wilderness of fallen trees. I'd been unsure of my position but when I broke through into the open, heralded by a fierce crack of thunder, I was more or less where I intended to be, on the crest of a long, open ridge. From there I proposed to walk the length of the ridge to the Col de Turini, where there appeared to be a ski centre and therefore accommodation. It was wild country with great boulder fields and a few gnarled trees on my right, in contrast with the heavily forested slopes I'd just passed through.

I scrambled over several outcrops of rock until I was stopped short by a considerable barrier, twenty feet of sheer wall. The French mark their walking routes with paint, and slap in the middle of this rock face was a daub of red. The trunk of a little tree perched on top was also splotched with red. It was clear enough – the way to go was straight up. But how?

This spot is known as the Tête de Gaglio, which may mean the galleon's prow. It looked like one. I thought it would be feasible if a rope could be got to the tree but I didn't have one and wouldn't have known how to use it anyway. There were plenty of holds for a rock climber, but not for me, and especially with a heavy pack on my back. I gingerly explored one or two handholds but the thought of a body lying at the foot of the cliff in a twisted heap was enough to deter me. Besides, what horrors might lie beyond?

I searched for a way round but there seemed to be no easy way to turn the obstacle. So I broke into the forest again and forced my way down, snagging my pack at times, clambering over trunks or squeezing under them, and at last I came upon the bulldozed track.

I was a sorry sight when drenched, muddied and bedraggled I arrived at the Col de Turini. On the col were a handful of hotels, auberges and ski apartments, nearly all closed. At the first open door I took off my sodden boots and padded in wet stockings over the carpet to reception, where I demurred at the price of a room. The clerk suggested a cheaper place next door and there I was soon established in a small room facing a red sunset over a foreground of dark trees. The sky cleared, mist rose from the valleys, birds began to chorus.

'Does it always rain in the afternoons?' I asked the woman folding napkins in the dining room.

'It does'.

But next day it didn't. When I reached a grassy summit topped by a ski pylon the views of blue and snowy hills on the horizon were spectacular. There I'd be before the week was out, I promised myself.

In the meantime there was no hurry. After the previous day's exertions I proposed an easy day. The sun was shining when I entered a green leafy lane in the forest and met a young woman striding along with two dogs, and it was still shining at the end of the day when I came down towards the village of Moulinet and, to my surprise, met the same woman and her dogs, barking to see me again. I remarked on her speed.

'I live here', she said. 'I know short cuts'.

I think Moulinet has more wynds, pends and vennels in a short space than the High Street of Edinburgh. I stopped just outside at a tall farmhouse speckled with numerous green-shuttered windows. In the field a man with a shaggy black beard like a brigand's paused as he fed a flock of goats and shouted for his wife Antoine. Later, as he sat hunched over a table in a pool of candlelight with a green bottle of wine in front of him he looked more like a bandit than ever. Antoine showed me to a bare room with a tiled floor, sink with cold water, and a mattress on a bed frame, and broke the bad news that there would be no evening meal.

'If only you'd come earlier . . . ' she said.

So I went down to a pub in the square where men in check shirts were playing cards noisily under a sign at the bar: *Buvez Choky, arome do cacao*. No Choky for me, I'll drink beer. A tall, elegantly shaggy dog that might have passed for a wolfhound in the colour fawn, approached the door in an aristocratic way, stood on his hind legs and, laying a nonchalant forepaw on the handle, opened it.

'Why doesn't he shut it', a check shirt grumbled after the dog had gone.

Antoine did me wrong, forcing me out to dine. That meal was the worst I have eaten on French soil. The salle à manger was reached through a small sitting room behind the bar where a crone in black sat watching television. I tried to ignore the fat man at the next table who slurped and gulped as he shovelled his food. The main dish was a pink and underdone hamburger with cabbage which I forced myself to try, thinking I might need the protein. I was on the verge of conversion to vegetarianism at that moment.

Tucked in my sleeping bag on the iron bedstead, lulled by the noises of a southern summer's night, I started to read the book I'd picked up downstairs, a yellow paperback by Dorothy Sayers called Lord Peter et l'Autre (Murder Must Advertise, I discovered later). With the help of a pocket dictionary, Lord Peter was to prove a good friend. Antoine insisted on making it a gift when I offered to buy it, and it lasted me as reading matter for the rest of the trip.

The brigand was milking his goats when we left. Antoine drove me in her jalopy van to the nearby town of Sospel, which lies on the river Roya in a valley to the east of the Vesubie. I climbed to the railway station and discovered that a train heading north towards the Italian frontier would leave in ten minutes, allowing me too little time to investigate two elegant old railway carriages I discovered at rest in the undergrowth of a deserted siding, bearing the magical words Orient Express in gold letters on their sides.

How did a portion of the fabled Orient Express come to a halt in this backwater of Provence? A notice indicated that to see the train one should contact a Monsieur Weiss on board, but of M Weiss there was no sign. I peered in at a few windows and saw a typewriter on a table in the saloon car and a bunk made up with a tartan rug in the wagon-lit, but no one was at home. I caught the incoming train, hoping that chance would bring me back to investigate, but it never happened. M Weiss and his share in railway legend remain a mystery.

12

Clarence Bicknell's world of wonders

Long tunnels, sharp curves, sheer hills and dizzy gorges characterise the way to Tende, latterly in an Italian train. Tende is a frontier town only a couple of tunnels away from the Italian border. Tiered against the hillside, it is a town of grey stone walls and slate roofs, of narrow streets, steep lanes and stony flights of steps flanked by mean doorways and shuttered windows, of secret nooks, poky corners and mysterious archways. No hint of the balmy Mediterranean here; Tende may be only thirty miles or so from the sub-tropical south but it's a far cry in the mind. Tende belongs to the mountains from which it is carved. I first saw it in the grey light of a dull morning and even in sunlight it retains a reserve. But the people redeem it. As I sat on a slate bench above the rushing river eating a sandwich, a little girl of about twelve with long blonde hair came by with her schoolbag on her back.

'*Bon repas, Monsieur*', she said with a perky smile. '*Bon appetit*'. And an old man at his garden gate hailed me for a chat.

Perhaps because Tende is so close to Italy and lived for so long unwillingly under Italian rule, French nationalism is blazed on many walls. In the tiny Place Augustin Boin a plaque records that citizen Boin was mortally wounded by Italian carabinieri on September 17, 1945 – after the war had ended – for shouting '*Vive la France*'. Other memorials were simply inscribed '*mort pour la France*'. There's a Place de la Résistance and a Rue des Disparus en Russie. A more recent and bloodless campaign is recorded in fading letters on the parapet of the high viaduct that carries the railway over the gorge. I could just make out the slogan *Non au parc contre le volonté des Tendasques* – people of Tende say no to the national park. Another graffito at the station was less clear in its message: *Tende aux Tendasques*, Tende for its own people, which I took to be aimed at white settlers looking for holiday homes.

Sitting in the Café du Centre waiting for the Gîte les Carlines to open, I studied a sensation in the newspaper. Nice-Matin reported a bizarre aerial accident that had killed the stuntman and sky diver Alain Prieur, with coloured graphics showing the stages in his fall. Prieur, out of bravado not wearing a parachute, had planned to descend a rope from one glider to another, but when he reached the end of the rope the second glider was not in position. Strength failing, he let go and plummeted until miraculously an assistant, a free-fall parachutist, swooped down and caught him in mid air. As they clung together the rescuer clipped Prieur to his own harness. They fell linked together until, fast approaching the ground, the rescuer had to open his parachute. The jerk tore the clip apart and Prieur fell to his death.

A bit shaken by this graphic account, I finished my coffee and walked up to explore the cathedral, which was soothing. It's small as cathedrals go. A row of saints guards the doorway, and though the windows are gothic the interior is ornately baroque. Dingy old paintings, difficult to see properly in the crepuscular gloom, hang on the walls under a vaulted roof spattered with faint stars. The waxy smell of candles mingles with a whiff of mould.

I shared residency at the Gîte les Carlines with a couple from Paris. Huguette and Jacques Dedieu were snug in a bedroom to themselves and I bunked in an eyrie overlooking the gorge. Jacques was considerate: would I prefer not to talk? (I was reading Dorothy Sayers in the kitchen). Of course I'd talk – I always do. So began a long and halting conversation with the Dedieus (a surname that means 'from God'). Jacques was patient and took pains to articulate clearly and, in a kindly, rather schoolmasterly way, to correct my French. The Dedieus were at the start of a four-week holiday roaming the local hills, in preparation for which Huguette boiled up a king-sized pot of spaghetti. Jacques swore by spaghetti. It would give them slow-burning energy all next day, he said.

In the morning our ways parted. I followed a road upwards by hairpin bends. There were views down the valley into the villages of Brigue and St Dalmas far below. The asphalt road dwindled to a dusty track and then to a woodland path. Below I could hear the sound of a rushing torrent magnified by the steep sides of the ravine, and occasionally I caught sight of cars on a narrow road that led to a spot marked on the map as Les Mesches, where two valleys meet at the Lac des Mesches.

Nearing the lake, the path left the woods and crossed an exposed and somewhat precipitous rock slope. The path had been paved and shored up here and there by retaining rubble, and at times a ledge had been blasted out of the solid rock, as drill holes showed. A swift descent led me to the lake, a large green pond set among pine trees, dammed at one end and glinting in the mist, a typical example of the French habit of building industrial sites at beauty spots. Wherever there's a convenient gorge they'll squeeze in a power station. The charm of the place was degraded by industrial buildings, including a gaunt concrete framework which had been left unfinished, or abandoned, or perhaps was in the course of demolition. Around lay deserts of spoil over which I had to walk to regain the track that would take me to Neige et Merveilles.

Snow and wonders. There was no snow when I arrived, just green grass and bare rock. Neige et Merveilles is a cluster of rough stone buildings built higgledy-piggledy on terraces at the head of a valley. At one time it had been a mining settlement (hence its map name La Minière) and a great rusting iron wheel, a relic of mining days, lay propped against a wall.

A woman carrying a plasterboard and trowel appeared. Her French was as dodgy as mine – she was Czech – but she managed to direct me to the office where I found Heleen from Amsterdam. Neige et Merveilles was beginning to appear like a united nations. Heleen enrolled me for thirty francs as a temporary member of the Association Neige et Merveilles and offered a simple choice of rooms: basic or comfortable. I chose comfort and full board at 170 francs a night, to stay as long as I desired. My room was in a tall block that looked like a barracks, which in fact it once had been. A unit of the Italian army had been billeted there in the war. The comfort was relative. The room was a bare box with a double bed, with blankets but no sheets, a wash basin, a small wardrobe, a thin felt carpet and a small window looking on to a waterfall. There was a heater but it didn't work. From time to time I switched it on hopefully, for it was chilly in the evenings, but without any result. In fact the heating had just been turned off, since according to the calendar it was summer.

That night I met the founder of the community. I never learned Monsieur Hirzel's first name. He called me John but I was always formal. I think I was a little awed by him. Not that he was gruff or unapproachable, merely that he seemed a little aloof, even when he sat by the fire in the bar surrounded by his young volunteer workers from many lands. He'd push his spectacles back on his white hair and listen amiably to the talk, seldom saying more than a word or two himself. The same happened during meals, when he sat benevolently at the head of the table.

M Hirzel was working as an engineer when he and some friends discovered the ruinous buildings at La Minière, which they bought and set about restoring, with the idea of founding a community to share a simple, labouring life in the mountains. The project changed character as the building work advanced, summer by summer, with a task force of volunteers from troubled parts of the world. At first, after the war, many of them came from Germany, then in the sixties from Africa, and more recently from eastern Europe. Apart from the satisfaction of the task itself – hard, outdoors work with a touch of idealism about it – the venture was now designed to provide accommodation for visitors wishing to explore the surrounding country, and particularly the prehistoric carvings found in the valleys to the north.

It was Jean-Marc, the young, bespectacled project manager, who first told me about Clarence Bicknell. Bicknell, he explained, was an Englishman who had lived in the area and was the first to make detailed records of the figures and symbols carved in great numbers in the upper parts of these valleys. Many carvings were of weapons, particularly daggers, and the heads of horned animals. They are reckoned to have been made during the Bronze Age, but it's not known for what reason. Since these valleys radiate from the central pile of Mont Bégo, a dark and brooding mountain thought to have had a mystical or religious significance, the carvings may have been made as an offering or propitiation to the gods who lived there. Bégo could well be imagined as a home of the gods. According to Jean-Marc it is a focus for electrical storms. Thunder and lightning often play around it, perhaps attracted by the minerals it contains.

I saw few of the carvings, partly because so many of the rocks were under snow and partly because I wasn't sure exactly where they were and was usually more concerned with route-finding than archaeology. They're not works of art, no mighty creatures with curving flank and flaring eye. At the top of a pass I found a whaleback of rock gouged by glacial action on whose concave side countless stick figures had been cut, so shallow they barely made an impression on the surface. They showed grey against the yellowy brown of the rock. I saw others in the neighbourhood, along with a number of graffiti added down the centuries, from the Middle Ages to the present. On a wall of rock accessible to the path, among glazed rocks blackened by dribbling waters and jewelled with tiny star-like flowers half hidden in the crevices, the scribblings of the moderns outnumber the old engravings.

Clarence Bicknell devoted many months over many years before and after the turn of the century to tracing and recording these rock engravings. Bicknell first entered the Val des Merveilles in the month of June, and because of the heavy snow he saw little on a brief visit. Four years later, in September 1885, he returned, spent the night at La Minière, presumably in one of the mine houses, and was able to sketch about fifty engravings. Then he began to visit in earnest, at first motivated by his interest in Alpine botany but also to investigate the carvings.

Hearing that a house was to let in Casterino, a hamlet (now a ski resort) in a neighbouring valley, he decided to spend the summer there. With his Italian friend Luigi Pollini, who was to be his companion on subsequent expeditions to the Merveilles, he

sketched more and more of the engravings and then, arming
himself with large sheets of paper which he bought in Tende and
carried up to the mountains, he started to take rubbings from the
rock. Year after year Bicknell and Pollini returned, often camping
overnight in the high valleys, until Bicknell had amassed a
comprehensive collection of sketches, rubbings and photographs
and had become an authority in learned circles.

When the house he had rented was sold, he had a chalet built
in Casterino on ground belonging to an Italian nobleman, the deal
being that on Bicknell's death the chalet would revert to the
landowner. In the following years he combed the Val des Merveilles
and the neighbouring valleys, probing deeper into their recesses,
climbing ever higher among the peaks (with Pollini doing the leg
work when the ageing Bicknell felt the strain), and discovering a
huge number of engravings. The work was more or less complete
when he died in 1918.

Though he gained a reputation in scholarly circles and wrote
a small book about his discoveries, Bicknell is a shadowy figure. He
is not recorded in the Dictionary of National Biography. The
volume he published in 1913 has long been out of print, though
French and Italian translations were printed to mark the fiftieth
anniversary of his death. I bought the French version during my
stay at Neige et Merveilles.

According to M Hirzel, Bicknell was pastor to the English
community in Nice, and also an amateur botanist. When he had his
house at Casterino built he painted flower murals on the walls,
which M Hirzel had seen in the days when the landowner allowed
the house to be opened to visitors once a year.

I set off for Casterino to have a look at the house, if only
from the outside. It was a Saturday and fishermen were lining up in
the meadows alongside the river and round a little lake whose
placid dark green waters were fringed by pine trees. It was hot and
sunny and my boots, soggy from walking in the snow the day
before, dried on my feet as I tramped along the road. Casterino
proved to be a settlement of three hotels, a shack offering mountain

bikes for hire and not much more, set in pastures edged by mountains and curtained here and there by mature woodlands. Not finding any obvious sign of Bicknell's house, I enquired from the lady at the Marie-Madeleine hotel.

She directed me through tall larch trees just sprouting with fresh shoots, and in an overgrown clearing I found the house; Casa Fontanalba, it was named in Italian on a plaque on a side wall, 'built in 1905 by Clarence Bicknell, principal discoverer of the Marvels of Mount Bégo'. The plaque, put up to commemorate the fiftieth anniversary of Bicknell's death, recorded (now in French) the gratitude of the peoples living on both sides of the Alps and their pledge to European fraternity. But the house doors were closed and the windows shuttered. Casa Fontanalba – or at least its owner – does not welcome visitors.

M Hirzel thought the Maison Bicknell typically English. I could have imagined it in Anglo-India, the sort of home a planter or colonial officer might have built as a retreat in the hills. It has two storeys, with a high timber verandah at first-floor level. The shallow tin roof extends to wide eaves shading the upper storey, and a chimney block stands like a pepper pot in the centre.

Clarence chose his site well. The house is secluded and there are views through the trees to hilltops all around, many of them, at that season, patched with snow. Nothing can be seen of Casterino, which in Bicknell's day must have been little more than a few peasant dwellings. Curious to see more, I wandered round the house and tried to peer in, but without success. In front of the house there is a low retaining wall of rough stones, forming a narrow terrace, and near it a little burn tumbles noisily down the hillside. Bicknell described in his book hiring labourers to build this wall and divert the stream closer to his home.

No one lives there from one year's end to another, which seems a pity. I gave Clarence my silent homage and set off to climb Mont Angelino, the hill that rises prominently across the valley opposite the Maison Bicknell's french windows.

Half way up, the grassy slopes were dotted with wild flowers and shaded here and there by groves of trees. From that level I could look down the long valley that carries a road towards distant Tende. Then I followed a cart track that zigzagged upwards, sometimes submerged by an overflow of snow, and through a narrow pass between rock pillars called La Porte. Near the top, a line of beehive forts or gun emplacements had been built into the mountainside, each with a rusty chimney pipe sticking from its rubble dome.

The hilltop was jumbly and stony, and distinguished only by the panorama of jagged blue peaks it offered. Turning to look behind me, I saw the dark mass of Bégo, a fissured black wall almost sheer except for diagonal ledges mantled with snow, and, fascinated, I stopped time and time again on the descent to look across at it.

From then on, Bégo was always in my sights. I got nearer it next day when I walked up the Vallon de la Minière. A couple of jeeps were parked at a holiday home, and nearby a woman and two men sauntered through the grass with their heads bent and eyes on the ground. I guessed they were looking for mushrooms. At the head of the valley Bégo hunched a bare shoulder, with a swathe of snow at the top.

I hopped across river boulders and started to climb a hillside. The ground grew stonier and I saw three chamois grazing above me, under a cliff. They were aware of my presence and occasionally lifted their delicate, horned heads, until I was thirty yards away and they took swiftly to their heels. I heard the shrill cry of marmots but saw none; they were probably hidden in their burrows among the rocks. I'd hoped to see moufflons, a shaggy, brown-coated goat-like creature with long twisted horns; Jean-Marc had said they were about, but I was unlucky. Moufflons, ancestors of the domestic sheep, are back in these hills after a period of absence, reintroduced from Corsica after being hunted to extinction.

I climbed to a rock prow overhanging cliffs, making heavy weather of it, which I put down to the effects of height – though it was less than 8,000 feet. From there I could look straight into the

black face of Bégo, to be reached, as far as I could tell, only by
narrow chain of pinnacles and towers. I didn't fancy that, so I took
an easier option and sat down to eat my lunch. Then I retraced my
steps to a pass, the Gia de Valauretta.

Here the ground dropped sharply, and the scene changed
abruptly from summer back into winter. On one side of the pass,
green grass and a profusion of wild flowers; on the other, barren
rock and snow. I was looking down into the Fontanalba valley,
another site where rock carvings abound and Clarence Bicknell had
been busy. The slopes shelved down in pavements of rock, smooth
and dark, with wide snowfields. Two torrents gushed down to a
little lake, slate green in colour (hence the Lac Vert de Fontanalba),
surrounded by a fuzz of bare larch trees.

The lake was tempting and I decided to explore it. It was
further than it looked and the steep path was submerged in places
by great wedges of soft snow. Having reached the lake, and not
wishing to clamber up again, I set off down the wooded Vallon de
Fontanalba to Casterino, where I joined the familiar road home for
a last night at La Minière. I reckoned it was time to try the higher
hills again.

'And so, Monsieur John', said M Hirzel, 'you are leaving the
delights and comforts of Neige et Merveilles for living rough in the
mountains'.

Flights of mosquitos, a sign of warm weather, spurred me on
through the open woodland and water meadows of the Minière
valley. I was defenceless against them. The Knoydart snorer's bottle
of Bug Off was buried deep in my pack. Only higher ground
brought relief.

I had a choice, either to follow the cart track which took an
easier, winding line, or climb by a rough track through the Vallon
d'Enfer. No question, it had to be Hell Valley. The challenge was
irresistible.

The jaws of hell closed over a stream raging through a
wilderness of boulders and scrub. In truth it was a half-cock sort of

hell, picturesque rather than frightening. It opened into a broader landscape of stone and scant vegetation, hemmed in by a ring of tortured peaks. Three lakes lay in this basin, the Lac Saorgine, the Lac Long Inférieur, and largest of all, the Lac Long Supérieur, beside which stood the Refuge des Merveilles where I hoped to spend the night. There was room at the inn and a meal in prospect, so I dumped my rucksack and made for the nearest peak, a craggy hill called the Cime des Lacs.

I failed to find the path shown on the map. Probably it was masked by snow in the gullies. So I veered round behind the hill into a wide rocky corrie overhung by a bare cliff. I scrambled over boulders, trying to spot a practicable approach, crossing scree and then heaps of tumbled rock until, near the top, I could pull myself over a turret that barred the way to the summit cairn.

Others had arrived at the refuge when I returned. There was a lively party led by a woman in a pink tracksuit, with her blond hair in a long pigtail. The sound of her loud whinnying laugh rang through the wooden-walled rooms at regular intervals. She turned out to be a professional guide. There was also a young French couple with the air of serious mountaineers, wearing plastic boots and carrying axes and crampons, and the man had a coil of rope looped on his pack.

We got talking.

'Are you Scottish?'- Yes I was.

'Were you at the Col de Turini the other day?'- I was.

'Were you in Moulinet? With Antoine and the brigand?' (but they didn't say brigand). -Yes.

They laughed. They'd followed in my tracks, a day behind, always hearing tales of a lone Écossais tramping the hills.

Two men and a woman staggered in, bowed down by massive packs from which spilled quantities of stores; big round loaves, bottles of wine, food and drink for the whole company. More provisions would be helicoptered in later but in the meantime everything had to be carried up on their backs. They sat talking to the gardienne beside a bulky, antique cast-iron stove with the brand name La Bourgignonne stamped on it. I looked forward to seeing this sonsy dame from Burgundy in action, but in the end our pork chops were casseroled in a modern stove using bottled gas.

We ate by candlelight at big wooden tables while outside boisterous youths who had pitched camp further up the valley ate, drank and played cards by the shifting light of their head torches. There was a fresh wind blowing and they were well wrapped up. I was glad to be under a roof.

Early to bed. I turned in at nine but wasn't the first. Others were already rolled in their bags and fast asleep.

Next day, Bégo. I tried to get to the foot of the mountain by walking along the top of the dam at the end of the lake, but half way across there was overflowing water and I had to retreat and make my way over the boulders below. Then it was a case of following a faint track which doubled back and back on itself over scree and boulder. Ravens were crying in the upper rocks, and from higher ground yet another little lake came into view, the Lac d'Huile, blotched with scummy snow and crazed ice.

My side of Bégo was mostly clear of snow until near the top. More testing were the heaped up rocks ahead, and I had to haul myself over large and rather exposed boulders to reach the summit, which is topped by a slender cross. From the top, said the gardienne, you can see the coast on a fine day, and when it's very clear, even Corsica. But not that day, for mist kept rolling in and the views were limited.

I didn't attempt the traverse, which the gardienne had described as 'un peu délicat'. But I made a detour and it was early evening when I returned, overtaking a party of walkers who'd come over a pass from the direction of Le Boréon, the village where a fortnight earlier I'd turned back from the high hills. The leader was a lean, tanned, athletic looking type in a green T-shirt. One of them, a gloomy, long-nosed man, was tottering under the weight of a large and lumpy pack (the lumps turned out to be tins) who was limping badly. He suffered in silence. I tried several times to engage him in conversation but it was a one-sided effort. He barely grunted. There were one or two older men and a couple of young women, a fat friendly character whose jolly face was framed in a rug of curly hair and beard, and a wiry man with a gruff voice that came from the region of his boots, who pumped my hand vigorously every time we met. Another of the group peered at the world from under a dark blue woolly hat pulled over his eyes. I never saw him without it, indoors or out. I wondered if he slept in it. This heterogeneous group were old friends who got together once a year for a mountain expedition.

By six o'clock in the morning people were creeping about the *dortoir*, folding kit and packing their sacks. In consequence I was out in the open and walking well before eight, though I wasn't the first. Ahead I heard the chatter and the whinny of the pink lady and her party, and I made haste to pass them.

The sun was still low and there was hard frost in the valley bottom. The cold urged me on over banks of snow which were now glazed with ice, quite unlike the sugary crumble of previous days. As the slope increased I was forced to hack steps with the axe, thinking that if I'd had crampons I could simply have walked on. I'm not used to cutting steps and I found it hard work and sore on the back. Had I been wiser I'd have waited for the sun to strike. Half an hour later I looked back from a height and was chagrined to see the pink whinnier with her group in tow, striding easily across the same snow slope which by then had been softened by the sun.

I was perched on a rock on the skyline at the Baisse (or pass) de Valmasque, where two valleys meet. The track leading up to this point was bunged up with snow and I'd mounted the rock to scan the other side, fearing there might be a cornice. But all was well. The snowy wedge came to a peak and then dipped down on the other side without any overhang, and I could simply kick steps over it.

I was now entering the valley of the Valmasque, a white waste in which three frozen lakes lay in line ahead under the Basto mountain (a name that means beast of burden). As I descended into

it, three figures approached from the north, two of them the French
couple I'd met at the refuge. They'd moved on to spend a night at
the Lac du Basto and were now heading for higher ground. Later I
looked back and saw them making good progress, just dots in a
white expanse with black rocks towering over them. The third man
was going into the Merveilles.

The snow was soft and deep in the valley. This was the time, I
judged, to try out the racquettes, or snow shoes, I'd hired at Neige
et Merveilles on Jean-Marc's advice. My trapper-style snow walking
was not a success. The unwieldy racquettes – rather like elongated
tennis rackets – were fine just clumping along on level ground, but
as soon as the slope increased they got in the way. After fifteen
minutes I took them off, strapped them back on my pack, and never
used them again.

I wanted to cross into the familiar Fontanalba valley by way
of the Baisse de Fontanalba. After a deal of dithering with compass
and map I chose the route which from ground level seemed to be
most direct and least encumbered with snow. I distrusted the snow
and tried to keep off it as much as possible, preferring to scramble
on the exposed rock. I had a dread of triggering off an avalanche
on the steep snowfield, now exposed to the strongest rays of the
sun. This fear was probably quite unfounded. It was old snow,
compacted over many weeks and would not slip – so I was assured
later. But I was uncertain of this at the time.

Once at the pass I looked over an expanse of snow, icy
lochans and denuded rock that shelved away in barren platforms to
the green dot of my old friend the Lac Vert de Fontanalba. No sign
of a beaten track met my eye. According to the map a path twisted
round under the black cliffs of Bégo's long eastern spur, but that
ground was covered in deep snow. A large block of snow as big as a
house lay among shattered debris at the foot of a gully, down which
it had rolled from higher ground. I decided it was not the way for
me, which left one course – to make a beeline down the open
ground. The destination, the Lac Vert, was clear enough. The route
seemed straightforward, except that there was no guarantee that the

general slope of the rock didn't hide the occasional abrupt drop. But I'd studied these slopes from below only a few days earlier and I felt confident I could chance it.

I saw a figure in a red jacket purposefully making his way across the rocks and I expected our paths to cross. From time to time his jacket and mop of black hair appeared against the snow, and lower down I followed his boot prints until they disappeared on bare rock. But where had he gone? It seems incredible that he could vanish in such a wild, empty, treeless quarter, but so it was. I never saw him again.

I wormed through fissures in the rock to where streams ran in grassy hollows towards the lake. The sun blazed, the snow glistened and I stripped by the lakeside, dipped my feet in the icy water, laid out my wet boots and socks to dry, and sunbathed for a little. Then I tackled my lunch, the usual half loaf and accompaniment, this time sausage. It was half-past one, six hours or more since I'd last eaten, but until then I'd not felt hungry. The excitement of the day's walking had kept appetite at bay. The scene was idyllic. But for the snow in June and the magnitude of the surroundings, it could have been Lakeland, with a green tarn fringed by tall larches and rugged hills.

The ascent to the familiar Baisse de Valaurette was arduous while it lasted, though much of the snow that had overlain the track on my earlier visit had melted away. Once I left the regions of snow and ice and entered the temperate zone on the other side I found many butterflies spreading their wings in the sunshine, some brown, others orange, black, yellow or white, and most of them intricately patterned. I regretted not knowing their names.

I wanted to return to the refuge by a track that according to the map contoured the hillside high above Hell Valley, but when I reached the point where it should have branched off there was no sign of it. Arrows pointed back up to the pass and down to La Minière, but there was a blank in the direction I wanted to go. I walked down to a stream and lo! there appeared ahead a miniature cairn, just two or three stones in a pile, and faint traces of an overgrown track. And beyond, another little cairn on a knoll. On rocks or trees I began to discover the occasional daub of green and yellow, badly faded and barely distinguishable. The way was marked after all. Always a spindly little cairn popped up at the right time to lure me on.

So I was led along winding ways with the torrent roaring far below, through boggy meadows with drifts of wild flowers. In these oozy beds were buttercups, violets (white, mauve and yellow), forget-me-nots, orchids, and many others I didn't know. I came to a rockfast desert where a few stone huts or *bergets* had been built for summer herding. Half way along, a little aerial care was needed when the track made a switchback turn on the edge of a cliff. I had a clear view, but it must have been at this spot – as I learned that night – that two walkers had gone astray in mist two years before and fallen to their deaths. Since then the path had been abandoned and the markings removed, which accounted for my initial puzzlement. It was only when I retraced my steps the next day that I noticed a warning: *Dangereux. Sentier dérouté* – Dangerous, path abandoned. I don't know how I'd missed the warning in the first place but I'm glad I did.

My reason for returning was the vain hope of finding my spectacles. In the neighbourhood of the bergets I'd wanted to look at the map and I reached for my glasses. Not there. I tried all my pockets, I tried the pack, but the spectacles had gone. I must have dropped them somewhere on the way. This was a setback. Reading – and that included map reading – would be next to impossible. It was a severe handicap. Apart from navigation, finishing Lord Peter became a struggle. The diary I wrote nightly declined into a spiderish scrawl (temporarily improved when the gardienne lent me her spare glasses. I willed her to make me a gift of them but she didn't).

Before setting out on this fruitless search I'd spent the morning climbing the Cime du Diable, a 2,700-metre peak in the long north-south range that extends to the Italian border, notable for the wide views it affords. On the way I passed Green T-Shirt's party already strung out at wide intervals, some sitting by the dam at the Lac de la Muta, a stretch of water crusted with ice. Here my friend with the voice in his boots shook hands with me for the last time.

I perched for a good half hour on the stone table that crowns the summit of the Diable. The sky was clear and the panorama seamless. It was strangely peaceful. The fresh wind blowing in the valley had calmed. Wave upon wave of blue peaks rose out of misty valleys. Still no sight of the sea, alas, for all the lower ground to the south was shrouded in coastal fog. When I turned to go down I could watch the progress of Green Vest and Co as they traversed a long snow slope on a route that would take them ultimately into the Vesubie valley at Rockabilly. There were two stragglers. Through the glass I could see that one was limping and the other, in a green T-shirt, was jollying him along.

I spent one more night at the refuge in the high mountains. I returned to find La Bourgignonne had gone. While I was away the helicopter had called to land provisions and had whisked her away.

Next morning I left early and made my way back to Neige et Merveilles where I spent the rest of the day lazily reading (as best I could with a magnifying glass) and enjoying the sun. It was summer now and there was a holiday air the following day as I walked back to Tende. I encountered fishermen, backpackers and picknickers, and there were three jeeps parked at the trackside below a cottage. A large and noisy family was carrying up belongings as a man with a jerrycan poured petrol into one of the vehicles. All sorts of household goods were scattered on the verge, including a big shiny copper tureen with a bulging belly. Lots of potage in prospect. Half an hour later one of the jeeps rattled down past me, and two motorbikes came bumping up the rough track in quick succession, riders standing clear of the saddle. Suddenly there was dust, a smell of exhaust and the snarl of motors.

Further on I hit the road as it snaked downwards by a series of sharp bends, bordered by a tapestry of pink and white petunias. At a corner I met a biker standing by his machine, helmet in hand, gazing down over the valley into red-tiled La Brigue. He seemed surprised that I'd walked down from the mountains.

'I prefer an engine', he said. Then: 'How high are the mountains in Scotland?' He was not much impressed when I told him. 'Ah, but you have to climb them from sea level', I said.

Cars passed with the letter T for Torino on their number plates. Italians were crossing the border for the weekend.

Rounding a bend, I found the rooftops of Tende before me, grey houses splashed with ochre, terraced into the sweep of the valley, houses of mean aspect for the most part, fronted by galleries draped with washing. The pinky-orange cathedral tower with its plump dome rose above the slatey roofs. A walled cemetery crowned the village, filled with grand monuments wildly out of proportion compared with the cramped habitations of the living.

Having time to spare, I lounged in the bar of the Hotel du Centre reading a newspaper (pictured, the Nice triathlon, hundreds diving into the sea like lemmings) and watching Sunday traffic stream round the square outside and the heterogeneous cafe society within. An abrupt thunderstorm with a torrential shower reinforced the company. At the table next to mine three prim ladies sipped cups of chocolate. Standing by the bar a man with a weatherbeaten face, a pencil moustache and black greasy hair under his tricolour cap was in animated conversation with an old man in rough blue cardigan and sailor's hat. Bikers in bright gear sat at tables under the awning, with young locals in jeans lounging beside them. In came a familiar figure, seen on previous visits to the cafe, a large, paunchy old man dressed impeccably in shades of coffee and brown is if for the promenade at Nice. He settled down and unfolded Le Monde with fat fingers nuggeted with rings. I idly wondered if there was make-up on his saggy cheeks. Between us flitted the waitress, dark, petite, with filigree sleeves on her white blouse and a little black skirt drawn tight across her bum.

I left when the sun came out. The big black dog lying at the doorway stirred and rolled loopy eyes when I gave him a pat in passing. I walked up the narrow street towards the gîte, came to the cathedral and pushed open the door. To my surprise an audience was seated in the pews, all facing me. It was faintly surrealistic – felt like a scene from a Bunuel film. Then I realised they were not looking at me, but up at the organ loft where a woman sat at the keyboard. She played Frescobaldi, pure and ethereal, and then more bravura pieces, sometimes accentuated by tinny drumbeats and clashing cymbals. When the recital ended I snatched a word with her before she followed her audience out. She told me she lived in Nice and made a habit of touring the province playing on interesting old church organs. The organ at Tende had been built in the early nineteenth century, which accounted for the special effects – just the thing for Rossini.

I sat in a side pew as a shaft of sunlight stole across a gloomy painting of a suffering saint. Because some of the music had been melancholy, and the church too (churches often are) I thought sadly of Mary, my dear friend, dead. Tears came to my eyes. And when I left, I lost my way hopelessly in the narrow streets.

As night fell over distant snowy peaks, I sat on a wall in front of the gîte watching cars steam along the roadway in the gorge, heading back to Italy from the coast. Bikes revved and impatient drivers hooted behind a line of camper vans.

Lying in bed, alone in the house, I was sleepily aware of the cathedral's old bell striking the hours, and twice I woke to hear thunder.

13
A flame burns, a fire glows

The shoemaker's was shut. On the day that I needed him, Monsieur Sassallo the cobbler had deserted his last. Monday was his rest day.

They'd told me about M Sassallo at the mairie, though at first the girl at enquiries had been puzzled by my questions. Maybe I'd opened the wrong door. 'But what do you want?' she asked. 'This is the tax office'.

Shoemaker Sassallo was reputed to be a fund of local knowledge, but lacking his presence there were lots of things about Tende I never learned. I got some information from a white-haired man standing outside an antique store, a large shed filled with timber and old furniture, redolent with the scent of varnish and wood shavings. Yes, he confirmed, Tende had been Italian until after the war. He himself had been born in Italy. He married a local woman he met and fell in love with when he was stationed in the town with the Italian army. It was only since 1947 that French had been taught in the schools, but in any case most people spoke a patois that mixed the two languages.

I left Tende with regret. It had been my gateway to the mountains of the Mercantour, but now the best was over — or so I thought as the train coming from Italy carried me over the first of many viaducts on the way to gentler places in the south.

I alighted in Breil in the hope of buying spectacles. On the map it had looked a likely place. But Breil was a disappointment. Breil, when I found it, after having walked down the wide road in a drizzle of rain, was nothing more than a village deep in the curve of a river valley. Its handful of shops did not include an optician's. The clerk at the station had told me as much. He'd thumbed through yellow pages (the French, too, have yellow pages) and found no optician nearer than Nice or Menton.

There was no chemist, either. I thought I was in luck at the

stationer's, where I bought a magnifying glass with a battery
flashlight in it. But it was a dud. Something was wrong with the
electrics and it got alarmingly hot in my hand. So I threw it away.

Where to stay? Heavily laden again, I'd no desire to walk
far. I thought I'd find a place for the night, dump the pack and
maybe stroll up a gentle slope for the exercise. A gîte was marked
on the map. I entered a small, dark bar and asked the way.

'There's no gîte in Breil', said the woman at the bar. There
was a small pension, closed on Mondays (it was Monday). There
was also a hotel but it was too expensive. As a last resort she sent
me with a lame boy to ring the doorbell at the pension, just in case
Monday could be waived. But no one answered and the shutters
stayed shut.

I returned with the limping lad and ordered a snack.
Meanwhile a tall, black-haired young man appeared and I overheard
the woman – his mother, I think – discussing my situation.

He shrugged. 'There's a hotel', he grunted, and that was
that. I chewed my soggy croque monsieur (less appetising than
pictured on the gaudy menu on the wall) and brooded on the
waning attractions of Breil and its unfriendly bar.

Ironically, the pub had a garish mural of a peasant inn in a
romantic landscape, an image of bucolic jollity. Cheery villagers
slapped cards on the table, quaffed ale from flagons and smoked
their pipes contentedly. The reality was a far cry from this
fancy. The pub was like a grotto dedicated to the local football
team, Olympique de Marseille. The walls were festooned with blue
and white favours, plus team photos, and a blue heart overprinted
with '*J'aime l'OM*'. There was also a large portrait of Marseille's
high profile chairman Bernard Tapie, whose shady business deals
were about to be unmasked. I remembered earlier on the trip
watching Marseille being drubbed by Red Star Belgrade on TV, and
I took a retrospective pleasure in this. In Breil I became a Red Star
fan.

Apart from football, another sport was celebrated on the pub
walls, where several hunting pictures hung. One photo (circa 1950)

showed a group of sportsmen grouped around three dead boars. Another, labelled Retour du Chasse (1972) pictured more grinning men and their dogs. And an undated photo showed happy hunters surrounding the carcase of a wolf, between whose lifeless jaws a joker had placed a dead sheep. That settled it. Breil and I must part.

Kind fate steered me to the village of Saorge. Even the name is grateful to my ear, a sound that slides smoothly from the lips to the back of the throat and then forward again, SA-OR-GE. Say Saorge and feel good.

I could have taken the train on to Sospel and looked up M Weiss on his Orient Express. I could have headed straight for Nice and basked in the sun. But with the map spread out on the bar table I pictured Saorge only a few miles away on its hill above a curve in the Roya gorge. My morning train must have passed near it. Perhaps I'd even had a fleeting view between tunnels. It was walkable in an afternoon: the decision was made.

It took hours longer than I'd thought. Breil hardly seemed to budge as I looked down on its red rooftops from the climbing path. I was glad of a gurgling rivulet beside stone chalets. Cool water scooped up in the hands gave welcome relief from the heat. The grey walls of Saorge on its hilltop soon came into view, like Lhasa the forbidden city with snow-capped mountains beyond, but it seemed to be as inaccessible. I was sorely burdened in the heat of the day and I'd failed to appreciate the lie of the land. All those kinks in the map (which I'd ignored) signified a constant succession of deep gullies to be crossed. In this terrible terrain anything short of a straight line on the map means trouble. Down steep gravelly slopes I'd go to rocky bottoms, dried-up tributary beds, only to clamber out again through thick and thorny undergrowth. The corrugations continued for several miles before I turned the corner on a rocky crest, descended to the roadside, hopped across stepping stones in the stream and began a last, long climb to the village.

By then it was evening. Two men talking in their gardens, as I approached by a broad grassy track, told me there was a hotel and – music to my ears – a gîte on the far side of the village, beyond the convent. Hot, parched and weary, I trudged past the demure Hotel Bellevue (tempting, but closed. Monday), up a street called Repentia, suitable for a convent, and along a country lane towards a tall, thin building with walls of rough-hewn stone, standing like an exclamation mark on the hillside.

I pushed open the heavy wooden door and entered a large, untidy and bare kitchen. There were red tiles on the floor, a handsome old dresser against the wall, a massy sideboard of the same vintage and a colossal, long table made from solid timber four inches thick. At the far end of this table stood a young man with the look of a reconstructed hippie, with a paintbrush in his hand and a pot of white paint beside him. He introduced himself as Frank, the *gardien* of the gîte.

Frank was short and sturdy and wore thick grannie glasses, had a mass of black curls on his head and stubble on his chin. Strictly speaking, he said, the gîte wasn't yet open for the season, but he'd already put up another walker for the night and I could stay too. In the middle of the room a screen of old balusters enclosed a stairwell with a spiral staircase (*un escalier en colimaçon*, as I knew from Lord Peter et l'Autre – the murder had been committed on such a staircase) which led down to the bunks. I dumped my sack by a little window giving on to a wooded valley, and without more ado, not even stopping to wash the sweat from my face, I ran back to village to quench my thirst.

The bar, of course, was closed. But there was a cafe overlooking the valley which provided cold drinks. Actually it was the bibliotheque, the village paper shop and lending library, but it had a fridge with cans in it and a table or two outside, so I was able to buy my first beer ever in a library.

When I returned, Frank was in the kitchen talking to a tall, rangy man dressed in a blue singlet and shorts and trainers. The newcomer's skin was burned mahogany by the sun, and he was just back from an evening jog.

'This man's a professional', said Frank admiringly. In due
course I came to think him eccentric, and maybe even slightly mad.
   René was a singular character. He must have been fifty, he
was lean as a rake, and his calf muscles were like whipcord. For
more than two months he'd been running round the map,
methodically following the numerous randonnée trails in the region
signposted and maintained by a body called the Conseille Generale
des Alpes-Maritimes. This wasn't for fun. The French trails are
carefully signposted and documented in a series of
guidebooks. René had set out to bring the guidebook information
up to date, correcting errors, noting missing or misleading signs, and
providing any additional information he thought necessary. It was a
self-imposed service to the community. No one had hired him,
though he had some idea – based more on a hope than a promise, I
fear – that the Conseille Generale might give him a fee in the
end. Running light, dressed only in his vest and shorts, with a
satchel-cum-bumbag round his waist, he covered huge distances. In
the past fortnight alone he'd totted up 500 kilometres and he
reckoned it would take him another six weeks to finish the job.
   René's preparations for his evening meal were meticulous. He
brought a carrot from his bag which he sliced wafer thin and spread
out raw on a plate with a sprinkling of oil and vinegar. Then he
cooked some pasta with butter and a herb sauce, and finally,
delicately turned a crêpe in a pan. After this simple meal – a kind
of scratch nouvelle cuisine – he took a large sheaf of papers from
his satchel and spread them neatly over the table. It was getting
dark, but Frank had gone to the village and at first we couldn't find
the light switch.
   'I must have light', he said as we searched for the oddly
placed switch (it was behind a beam). 'I've a lot to do'.
   I watched him with fascination for some time as he read
through notes he'd made on the run, checking them carefully
against his maps.
   The next morning he was at his paperwork again, and when I
left at eleven o'clock he was still busy. Frank told me afterwards that

he hadn't paid for his night's accommodation – he said he'd no money but would post it when the Conseille Generalle paid him. Frank was sceptical but philosophical about this dubious offer. René amused him – and he was certainly broke. The night before, René told me, he'd slept in a barn with rats for company and he hadn't eaten all that day. I do hope the Conseille Generalle came up with the money. He deserved it.

I stayed two nights at Saorge. In the morning I set out for my last walk in the hills. I had the square church tower in view for a long time, and a short stretch of railway line between tunnels on which the red-roofed Italian trains made a brief appearance on their way south. Sky-blue butterflies flitted among flowers at my feet as I walked through tall clumps of lavender. Below me a hillside flared with yellow broom and on the far horizon blue hills were stacked in tiers.

I turned away from a misty peak, preferring to stay in the sun, and scrambled down from a col where soil and vegetation were scarified by the hooves of many sheep on their annual summer expedition to high pastures. In error, I had turned away too soon, and spent the next couple of hours in the deep shade of the forest instead of walking high and clear on a track that traversed the stony hillside above. I was sunk in the Vallon de la Fontaine Froide (Cold Spring Valley) but the source was dry and only mossy rubble and dry boulders marked the course of a seasonal stream. Here and there laburnum trees in full bloom dangled yellow tresses.

I arrived at the village of Fontan, the neighbour of Saorge, and there made another mistake. Over a cool drink at a roadside cafe, watching the traffic speeding towards the black mouth of a tunnel, I judged that it might be hazardous to enter the tunnel on foot (there was no pavement) and that the only practicable walking route was a track that diverged from the roadway to zigzag up a long and steep ascent through the forest. It was still the full heat of the day. Now and again a fallen tree barred the route, so regularly and effectively that I was convinced it had been done deliberately – it was a struggle to clamber over the heavily branched obstacles.

Had René come this way, and would he submit a critical report to the Conseille Generale? I was weary and disgruntled when I arrived at Frank's, and even more so when he told me I should have boldly taken the short-cut through the tunnel.

'Everyone does', he said. 'It's only ten minutes'.

Frank had perched his two little children, Flavie and Felix, on top of the table and was singing to them as he played a guitar. A tape was playing in the background. He was embarrassed and stopped short when I came in.

'Do you know American?' he asked.

I said yes, sort of.

He switched the tape on again and together we tried to decipher the words, not easy because the anonymous tape was faint, distorted (and probably copied, I suspected). Who was the singer? It was impossible to say. We played it back countless times until at last intelligible scraps seemed to emerge, which he copied into a notebook.

> *I've got to know before I go,*
> *Does that flame still burn,*
> *Does that fire glow?*

I promised to identify the singer and the song, if I could, and send him the full text once I got home, but try as I might I failed. None of the music folk I knew could identify the song or the singer.

I said goodbye, and this time I took to the tunnel. I was nervous in the dark with only a pinpoint of light ahead, but the road was quiet and no traffic thundered past. Fontan-Saorge, the station midway between the two villages, is no more than a halt but it was built for the railway age and now has an air of neglected grandeur. An orange stucco palace on the outside, it was silent as a church indoors. Not a soul was about, inside or out, so I sat on a low wall on the platform and enjoyed the sunshine. A blue police van turned into the station courtyard and two shirt-sleeved gendarmes got out.

'Bonjour', we said, and a few more pleasantries. Then what appeared to be an interrogation commenced.

What was I doing? Where was I going? What was my name? Was I a tourist? and finally, 'Your papers, please'.

I handed over my passport which they studied briefly. All in order. They bade adieu and drove off, and I never learned what misdemeanour had been suspected.

Sunlight hammered into the train as it trundled down into the blistering heat of the Mediterranean coast, and I dozed as the fields of Provence rattled past the window. I had a shower in the station at Nice, wedged my rucksack in a locker and went for a stroll, marvelling like a backwoodsman (which I was) at the crowds – so cosmopolitan, sophisticated and chic – at the noise and smell of the traffic, at the hardness of the pavements and at the brilliance of the shop windows. There was, I observed ruefully, an optician's in every block with shelf upon shelf of spectacles on display. Too late.

I found my way to the sea, a vivid margin of ultramarine inshore turning to deep cobalt blue beyond. Big white cruisers cleft the water and a jumbo jet curved into the sky. There were swimmers in the bay and sunbathers on the beach, and the air was heavy with the scent of sun oil wafting over the promenade.

And in Paris next day, en route for home, it rained.

14

On the crater's edge

Would I care to spend a week on a tropic isle? You bet I would. I went. I'd never heard of the Comoros, but on the map I found four dots in the Indian Ocean between Madagascar and the east coast of Africa. Grande Comore, the largest of them, is dominated by Karthala, an active volcano. Maybe it could be climbed?

The Comoros have had troublesome times: swept into Islam centuries ago, prey to slavers, visited by pirates (Captain Kidd sailed these waters), colonised by Europeans, the French in particular. Present confronts the past uncomfortably in the Comoros and their recent history has been melodramatic.

The six journalists in our party (it was a press trip) were kept up to date by Ali-Toiher, a former government minister (before one of several coups) and now tourist officer based at our hotel. This air-conditioned pleasure dome, patronised mainly by South Africans, was the main employer on the island and its chief source of wealth. Ali was slim and spruce, whether dressed in crisp shirt and white panama or in his kandou, the long white shift Comorean men wear to the mosque or to be smart.

Ali showed us the villa once owned by the island's man of destiny, the French mercenary Bob Denard, kingmaker for a decade on Grande Comore and by then whiling away his last years in France after a spell of uneasy exile in Pretoria. Denard's career as a soldier of fortune had taken him to Biafra, Angola, Gabon and Benin before he waded ashore on Grande Comore with a small gang of armed men in the mid seventies and overturned the sitting president – the leader who had won independence from France – in favour of a young radical. Two palace coups and two assassinations later Denard was finally thrown out after exerting a dubious influence from behind the scenes on the country's politics and economy.

Ali pointed out where Denard's sunken flagship lies in the shallows of an enclosed bay called the Trou de Prophete (the prophet's hideyhole) where, legend has it, the island's first Muslim converts sheltered from their oppressors. This former trawler on which Denard arrived with his scruffy invasion force is now a tourist attraction, a weed-bedecked and shell-encrusted haven for marine life.

While seafood grilled on a beach barbecue Tony Kaye, boss of the island's water sports business, a South African engineer adventurer and good friend of Denard, told me how he'd manoeuvred the scuttled vessel over the bar and into the bay, a considerable technical feat. Denard had been maligned, Kaye insisted. He was a good man; he was a gentlemen.

'Bob always stood up when a lady came into the room', he said. I didn't ask if he always stood up for black ladies.

The sun shone, the surf broke on spotless sand, ice cubes tinkled in the glass.

Karthala is 2,361 metres high, just under 8,000 feet, and untrustworthy. Twenty years ago molten lava breached its side and engulfed a village. Only a wide swathe of black boulders shows where the dwellings had been. One year before my visit Karthala blew its top, hurling rocks from the summit and gouging a huge new crater which filled with an ultramarine lake.

From sea level Karthala is undistinguished, seemingly nothing more than a dull green dome rising gently from the tropical forest, with no obvious peak and nothing to give it scale under the immense blue sky. First I tried to fly over it, but that reconnaissance came to nothing. Four of us squeezed into the single-engined air taxi piloted by Henri Béla, a rotund middle-aged French Biggles dressed in khaki drill who had been an airline pilot for Air France. We took off into a clear sky but a cloud cap hung over the mountain top and Béla wouldn't venture into the mist. Instead we wheeled about and flew over the coral reefs, sandy crescent beaches and green volcanic hills of Moheli, the smallest of the Comoros,

towards the third, the perfume island of Anjouan. Over Moheli,
Béla philosophised.

'Those people down there are damned lucky', he rasped in a
tobacco growl. 'I envy them. They have no stress. No one dies of a
heart attack'.

Why didn't he retire to Moheli and share in the good life?

'I like progress', he replied, thus demolishing the idyll. A
plane to fly, a business to run and bang! the heart attack.

Béla ran it fine on the return. At sunset barbed wire coils
were spread over the runway at Moroni, capital of Grande Comore,
to prevent night landings. Maybe they feared another Denard from
the sky. We touched down in the nick of time, just as the sun slid
below the horizon.

Next day I rose before dawn. At half past four I was alone in
the lobby with the stuffed coelacanth. The coelacanth is an ugly
fish, blue-backed and sharp in the teeth, a survivor from Jurassic
time which had been deemed extinct until local fishermen began to
drag them up from the depths of the ocean. While waiting for my
taxi I read the details from a notice on the glass case in which the
hotel's stuffed specimen was displayed. At five o'clock I was being
driven demon-like by Chauffeur (his name) along the narrow unlit
coastal road where people were already about, ghostly figures in the
headlights. When we met Hassan, my guide, he had bad news. We
were to pick up a French couple who wanted to join in the climb. I
felt a twinge of disappointment. I'd hoped to go solo with Hassan.

The French turned out to be not two but four. The verandah
of their villa was floodlit in the dawn like a stage set and on it stood
a table spread with a white cloth and set for breakfast. This looked
promising. I hadn't eaten and was hungry. But Hassan and I were
not invited. We sat in the car and watched them sit down leisurely
to coffee and baguettes.

No point in hanging around while they breakfasted. Hassan
and I drove up a narrow winding road until it petered out and
waited there impatiently, talking to the three local porters whom
someone had engaged to take the party's food, tents and sleeping

bags (it was understood we'd camp overnight) to the top. They were a lively group, a good natured stocky lad in blue jacket and torn singlet, grubby and smelling strongly of sweat, a muscular giant who introduced himself as Maître Physique, and a lean athlete whose name I couldn't make out – privately I christened him Slim Jim. They marvelled at the boots I carried ready to wear on the walk, passing them from hand to hand, feeling their weight and astonished at the fortune I'd paid for them. They wore the flimsiest footwear, just flipflops or trainers.

At last the French showed up with their guide in a pickup; two young couples dressed for a picnic in shorts and trainers, with an accumulation of baggage including a large unwieldy cool-box which made the porters mutter. Hassan and I put our heads together and struck a deal. We'd press on ahead and leave the French and their guide to follow.

We set off into the bush and had our last sight of clear sky for several hours as we plunged along a narrow track cut through lush and overhanging greenery. It was not yet eight in the morning and the dewy foliage soaked my socks and shorts, so that soon my bare legs were a pattern of cuts and small lacerations. Slim Jim, hoisting the cool box on one shoulder, set a punishing pace, and soon the sweat was dripping from my nose and chin like a tap. I took off the new white cricket hat I'd bought for the tropics and carried it in my hand, where it soon became daubed with mud.

The ill-defined path was made treacherous underfoot by a network of roots, knobbly volcanic rock and mud. Here and there it narrowed to a deep trench little more than the width of a boot. Black and rotting logs lay half hidden in the undergrowth and fallen trunks formed barriers which had to be scrambled over or ducked under. Slim Jim soon shed his flipflops and strode on over this unfriendly terrain in his bare feet. As for me, I was glad of my boots.

After ninety minutes without pause we came to a break in the thicket where an old lava bed tumbled down in a lumpy fall of slimy rock, and there we halted while Maître Physique and Slim Jim retraced their steps to locate the French party. A plan formed in my mind. We'd set out for a two-day trip but I fancied getting back that evening if we could. Hassan didn't demur. He said it was possible. He'd rather spend the night in his bed than on the mountain top.

And so when Slim Jim and Maître Physique returned we pressed on without delay. We reached a clearing with signs of former habitation − low black walls surrounding a grassy knoll, all overgrown with flowering shrubs, hydrangea bushes and leggy briar roses among them. To my eyes it looked oddly like the policies of an abandoned big house in the Highlands. This oasis, Hassan said, had been built by a merchant extracting timber from the forest. I heard later it had also been used as a refuge or halfway house for expeditions climbing Karthala − hence its name, La Convalescence. We convalesced briefly, stretching out on the turf and eating dry buns, squares of chocolate, and sharing a water bottle − what passed for my breakfast.

We resumed. The bush was interminable. Once again there was nothing in view; no horizon, no feature visible through the green canopy. When we broke free it was into a broader landscape of low shrubs like broom (I can't tell what it was − I'm no botanist) on dry arid soil which was dotted with clumps of a gemlike daisy pink star flowers. Sometimes the shrub was shoulder high, sometimes it reached to the waist. One area had been burned to a thicket of blackened spears, and finally the shrubs became festooned with a tracery of pale lemon-coloured moss or lichen. It looked to me like the deer moss of Scottish forests. The character of the ground changed too. Slabs of reddish rock appeared underfoot, still bearing daisy tufts, and then it changed again and soon we were treading on black crumbly lava, evidence that we were nearing the top. We scrambled down a steep bluff on to a level plain of ash, knowing that the working part of the volcano was barely a mile away. Slim Jim, Maître Physique and the stocky boy busied themselves making camp while Hassan and I, thankfully dropping our sacks, continued over rough, dusty ground along a cinder track. By half past one, after nearly six hours of ascent, we stood at the crater's rim. At our feet, the abyss.

This new crater of Karthala is said to be the biggest in the world, three kilometres round in ragged circumference. And yet, until a year before when the mountain blew, it had been solid ground. Deep in the crater's heart, far below, lay the lake, a vivid green streaked with whorls of white. Some half a mile away, across the depths, a cliff grander than any I'd seen dropped sheer into the crater, with pyramids of scree at its base. There was nothing to give it scale and I couldn't estimate its height, but it looked impressive. To the left, a grassy ridge led towards the highest point of the mountain.

We spent some time just looking, Hassan as impressed as I. Then we crossed an expanse of cinder ledges to the original crater, a desolate arena filled with a black sea of jumbled rock, a chaos from which rose columns of steam, and here too we lingered.

When we returned to the camp site the rearguard had arrived and tents were being pitched in the dustbowl. We stayed just long enough to eat green seed-filled oranges and take a drink of water – and to indulge in a little acrimony. A Frenchman was brusquely quizzing Hassan.

'Speak French', he demanded querulously (I heard the frustrated colonialist in his tone). 'I know you can speak French perfectly well'.

Hassan stood dumbly with his eyes downcast, in time-honoured fashion. He knew his place. I was embarrassed and moved out of earshot. I liked Hassan and felt resentful on his behalf.

Just before three o'clock we started on the descent – Hassan, Slim Jim, Maître Physique and I. The stocky boy stayed with the French and their guide, and Slim Jim and Maître Physique proposed to return next day to help with all their gear. We set a fast pace, conscious that time wasn't on our side. The sun would set at six and by half past it would be dark. We had to be out of the bush by nightfall. I didn't know what dangers there might be, but Hassan looked serious.

It was touch and go. Muddy glissades, toe-stubbing rocks, snaggy roots and clutching creepers threatened to upend us in our headlong rush. Sweat ran in rivulets. Twice I stumbled wildly and behind me I heard Maître Physique murmur '*Doucement*'. Once when I fell hard, face down in the undergrowth, he pulled me to my feet and after that I knew he was keeping a wary eye on me. He also kept plucking bunches of red guavas from the foliage and thrusting them into my hands. The fruit was juicy and tart and I ate greedily till my stomach rebelled, but still he pressed them on me. After meagre rations, a cornucopia. Not wanting to offend him, I resorted to storing the fruit in the crown of my new floppy cricket hat, which was already muddy and soon became stained a rich red as the juices flowed. That hat is now indelibly marked with Karthala.

Dusk fell.

'We have to hurry, Monsieur John', said Hassan, and I heard the unease in his voice. We upped the pace. It's surprising how much the naked eye can detect in the dark. Though the light was fading fast under the canopy of leaves I found I could still pick out rocks and roots on the trail.

Slim Jim veered off the track and disappeared and I wondered what he was doing as the crashing sounds of his progress grew fainter. Hassan and Maître Physique were unperturbed and some time later Slim Jim reappeared with a bundle of what looked like saplings on his shoulder. They were sugar canes, hacked from a plantation with his machete – a sure sign, I felt, that we had reached cultivation, if not civilisation yet. Slim Jim tossed the canes to the ground at a clearing and cut the bark off the ends, then gave me one to try. I bit into the raw woody flesh as the others did, but though there was at first a pleasant sweetness my mouth soon filled with fibres, and I had to spit them out.

The last light failed just as we reached a discernible track, stony underfoot and wide enough for a truck. It eased my nerves, worried as I was about being benighted in the forest. But the situation was bad enough. My strength was ebbing and I found myself trailing behind the others, weary and footsore. I'd no idea how far there was still to go. At times we glimpsed the far lights of Moroni and a freighter moored in the bay twinkling below, but they seemed dispiritingly distant. Then when my mood was gloomiest I heard a mutter of conversation ahead and we came on a clearing lit by the headlights of a lorry and a pickup truck. We could hitch a lift – we had transport! I clambered stiffly over the tailboard of the pickup and sank back into something soft and agricultural, the nature of which I preferred to leave in doubt (it proved to be innocuous, a load of upturned turves).

We coasted down the winding road and tumbled out in Moroni's central square. Hassan hailed a taxi and I sat with the driver in front (the white man's place!) while Hassan squeezed in beside other occupants in the back. A taxi ride in Moroni is a sociable event. Passengers come and go along the route and there is animated chatter all the time. We stopped to make a drop at the gendarmerie and then at the hospital, a down-at-heel concrete building of seemingly Dickensian squalor with a metal grille at the entrance offering sight of peeling walls and a long, dimly lit corridor in which visitors – and patients, for all I knew – clustered silently. I wondered what proportion of the sick walked out after treatment. Not long before, the resident priest had donated mattresses for every patient but within days they were sleeping on bare benches again. The mattresses had been spirited away.

Hassan's boss Christian was sitting on his verandah when we arrived at his home – muddy, scratched and tousled scarecrows – to be greeted gravely by a rather grand major-domo. I was given a cool beer after which Christian, dressed immaculately in an embroidered kandou, drove me along the dark coastal road back to the hotel. After a shower I was able to join my colleagues for dinner in the outdoors restaurant. They greeted me with some surprise, for I hadn't been expected until the following evening. In fact a great fuss was made. It was the first time anyone had climbed Karthala and back in the same day, so they said. I'm pretty sure this

is a fiction but I didn't protest over much. An announcement was
made from the stage. People came up and shook my hand.
Christian said the news was to be broadcast on the radio. I sat back
easefully and sipped a glass of wine, briefly a local hero.

Later that evening I sat alone at the poolside. Barbecue smells
drifted across, mingling with the perfumed night air. The pool
shimmered, lit from below. I could hear the breakers pounding like
heartbeats on the deserted beach. In the black sky were more stars
than I'd ever seen, with the milky way strung through them, a
diaphanous net. A dreadlocked black entertainer sang to his white
audience, backed by drums.

A high fence and guarded gate house insulated us from the
rest of the island, where the people lived in block shacks or huts of
woven matting. The Africa just a few hundred yards away from the
beach hotel seemed as distant as the stars in the sky.

15

After you, Amelia

A gondola in the lagoon of Venice. Seated, a Victorian lady,
sketching. Amelia Edwards lifts her eyes to the horizon beyond
Murano. That line of faint blue peaks – the Dolomites! (the
exclamation mark is hers).

Once Amelia had seen an artist's sketches of the Dolomites
her heart was won. Haunted by 'their strange outlines and still
stranger colouring I thought of them as every summer came round;
I regretted them every autumn; I cherished dim hopes about them
every spring'.

In July 1872 she and a companion set out to explore this
siren land, then a seldom visited region of peak and precipice in the
Italian south Tyrol. First by coach and then, when the going got
rough, on horseback; two English ladies in wide hats and heavy
skirts jogging side-saddle over high passes, with a disgruntled male
(less adventurous than they) hired to guide them.

Amelia, a single woman in her early forties, novelist and
contributor to journals, published her account as Untrodden Peaks
and Unfrequented Valleys. She had a keen eye and a lively turn of
phrase and when I came across the book – out of print for a
century until republished recently by Virago – I was lured. On an
impulse I booked a flight to Venice and took off with pack and
boots.

'We have Mayr's maps', she wrote, 'Ball's guide to the eastern
Alps, Gilbert and Churchill's book and all sorts of means and
appliances'. They took 'a small store of tea, arrowroot, and Liebig's
extract, a bottle or two of wine and brandy, a flask of spirits of wine
and an Etna' – this last being a proprietary travelling stove – 'but we
have not the slightest idea of where we are going, or of what we
shall do when we get there'.

No more had I. I took a couple of maps from Stanfords and

less than the basketful of gear that served the ladies. Hang the
itinerary – take the train as Amelia did and see where it leads.

'And now we are at Conegliano, the last point to which the
railway can take us'. The line, extended since then, brought me to
the small town of Calalzo where a flock of twittering schoolgirls
accompanied by two silent nuns alighted with me. Amelia and
friend – whom she discreetly identified only as L – continued by
carriage. The girls, the nuns and I caught the bus.

Thus the village of Pieve di Cadore, birthplace of Titian,
became my gateway to the Dolomites. Sitting on a wall in the
Piazza Tiziano, I studied a statue of the master, palette in hand,
brush poised, standing legs braced apart at his supposed easel.
Amelia had passed this way and admired the Titian in the church, a
madonna and child supported on one side by St Rocco displaying
the wound in his hand and on the other by St Sebastian pierced by
arrows; twa sair sancts. I hadn't brought the book and so I bypassed
the church, though I doubt if I'd have found the painting anyway –
it's probably in a gallery by now.

Could this be my way, this overgrown lane between two
gable ends? It soon came to an end in woodland, from which I
emerged on to a narrow road where there was a wayside inn. The
inn was closed but the innkeeper, sitting at a table out of doors,
invited me to share a bowl of peaches. Then he opened a bottle of
wine. What with the juicy fruit and the heady wine and some
forlorn attempts at sensible conversation by means of a feeble Italian
vocabulary plus gestures and grins, half an hour sped by.

We had a visitor. A large bearded man, overlapping his small
moped, stopped for a glass and a chat with Vittorio (mine host)
before remounting and chugging uphill. I was totally unable to
follow their talk.

Vittorio directed me on my way. I was to follow a track
beside a line of ascending ski pylons, at the top of which I'd find a
marked path to the Rifugio Antelao. Because it was early in the
season – early June – the rifugio (a mountain hut or hostel) would
be closed but I needn't worry. A bed would be found for

me. '*Ciao*'.

Under rocky bluffs and on rolling scree I picked wild flowers whose names I didn't know. I placed them carefully between my travel documents – the most suitable substitute for a flower press I could find – and I have them still.

At the rifugio there was a surprise. Guido, the bearded mopedallist, was the resident warden, and he was expecting me. This I'd failed to grasp at the inn. I found a bed, stowed my gear and braced myself for a cold shower – Guido explained apologetically that it would have taken an hour to stoke the boiler for hot water.

I came down to another surprise. Vittorio had arrived and was talking to Guido on the verandah. Tonight, they said, there's a party, a celebration for a friend's fiftieth birthday. Would I care to join them?

Vittorio, who did the cooking, prepared the best spaghetti dish I've tasted, crammed with scampi, lobster, mussels and seafood of all sorts. There were big bottles of a local wine and then coffee, poured into the same glasses and laced with grappa. And then more grappa, this time not colourless but rich, strong and so dark it was almost black. The birthday celebrant had a real taste for the grappa. A squat man with bottle-shaped shoulders to match the object of his desire, he got drunk in a very short time and began to punctuate his conversation with great windmilling gestures. The only one of the party I could have any real talk with was the youngest, who had a luxuriant ponytail and wore a gold bracelet on his wrist and a stud in his ear. We had basic German in common.

After the meal the plates were pushed aside and a noisy game took place. Two players stood facing each other and thumped a hand on the table, making a fist or extending one or more fingers or slapping the table with an open palm, at the same time shouting out a number. When one gained a point the other stood aside and someone else took his place. What the rules of the game were I couldn't guess, and no one has ever been able to tell me.

At last the party broke up, cars bumped away down the rough

lane in the darkness, and I turned in. In the early morning Guido
clattered off on his moto for a meeting in Pieve with his boss, and I
made a short reconnaissance. A clammy mist came ballooning up
from the valley, blotting out the world except for brief views to
distant ragged skylines. Two climates alternated eerily – chill where
the mist lingered and hot when the sun broke through.

Guido looked glum when he returned. One word was
enough to express his thoughts. Bosses!

'They've no interest in the mountains', he grumbled. 'It's just
a job for them'.

He shrugged. *'Mangiare'* – let's eat. Guido wasn't in the
Vittorio class as a cook but there was pasta followed by steak and a
salad, with coffee and the usual grappa. That's pretty good hill-
walking fare.

I shouldered my pack and waved goodbye. By the wayside
were clusters of gentians and shy fritillaries dangling dusty bells. On
turning a corner I met the mountain and it was an awesome sight, a
bare pyramid of grey rock with its top cut off by cloud. 'A
wonderful vision, draped in vapours and hooded in clouds, stands
suddenly before us!' – Amelia from her coach – 'We know at once
in what Presence we are. We know at once that yonder vague and
shadowy mass which soars beyond our sight and seems to gather up
the slopes of the valley as a robe, can be none other than the
Antelao'.

Oh for your words, Amelia. The Presence is before me and I
stand in reverence. All day it will draw my eyes, now filling the sky
ahead of me, now edging behind lesser hills, but seldom out of
mind.

For a time I turned my back on the Antelao as I followed a
will o'the wisp, a signpost pointing to the Piano di Cavalli
(whatever a piano might be – only later I discovered it was a plain)
that took me far from my preferred way. I scrabbled down a deep
grass-lined gully in the rain in order to find the route again, helter-
skeltered down, down, down on muddy tracks through endless
dripping woods, crossed a river to a military encampment and was

stopped by a sentry standing guard at a barber-pole barrier. He gave
me the bad news that the nearby rifugio was closed, and so I had to
tramp long miles on a hard road which took me back into Calalzo.

I'd come full circle. At the Hotel Ferrovia, the station hotel, I
found a bed for the night and ate a splendid dinner for which – as I
discovered after I'd left, on studying my bill – it seemed I hadn't
paid.

From laundered bed linen to sleeping rough. The next night
I spent under the stars. Twilight found me still scrambling up a
crumbly track, grabbing for holds among roots and sinewy scrub,
hoping to find a bunk in a mountain hut or bivacca I knew was
somewhere up there. Before darkness fell I found a patch of level
grass on which to lay out my sleeping bag. Off came boots and
socks, on went long johns, and I wormed my way inside. Supper in
bed was a mouthful or two of bread and sausage washed down with
cold water, and then I zipped myself in. But not for long. Though
it was chilly outside I was sweating in the bag, so I rose and stripped
off, bare skin fingered by a soft smirr of rain. From then on I was
drowsily aware of showers pattering on the cover. Waking with a
dry throat, I felt blindly for the water bottle and ugh! found a slug
crawling up it.

When I surfaced in the morning skims of mist hung over the
black cliffs around my head and jets of water coursed down the
clefts. Yet later when it was hot I searched in vain for a trickle of
water. The boulder-choked gullies I came to were dry. Where had
the rushing burns of the morning gone? Sunk underground in
limestone hollows, I suppose. On such a dry bed I walked up a
sloping rock, slipped on gravel and tumbled all the way down
again. I landed at the bottom bruised but not bloodied. I picked me
up, dusted me down and walked on.

Below, a valley patched with sunlight; above, grey cloudy
hills. Ahead there was a treacherous slope with no certain sign of a
track across it. I gingerly crossed on shifting sand, looking towards
niagaras of pale debris fallen from steepled crags, across which
chamois delicately picked their way, now and then dislodging a

clatter of stones.

Far away lay a town which I took to be Cortina. My objective was closer, the village of San Vito, which I reached as the clock on the grey church steeple struck twice, tinnily. Young soldiers from a nearby garrison were strolling in the street. I was tired and went into the church to sit in a pew under a big, dark painting of a saint in some distress. A Titian? I think not. Amelia and her friend L had passed this way with guidebooks on their laps, and didn't stop. Amelia would never pass a Titian by.

Next morning I left the village in a gentle shower. An old woman under an umbrella at her gate said *buongiorno*. A cyclist free-wheeled down the hill singing of *amore*. Blue and yellow flowers clustered in the tall meadow grasses. To my right rose the marvellous Antelao mountain, fairylike and rosy in the morning mist.

Later I drank cool water gushing from a corrugated iron pipe where the roadway came to an end, and later still I sat on a bench with other walkers outside a hut called the Scotter – a rifugio, ristorante and bar (closed) – and ate a hunk of bread. The Pelmo, the other big mountain of the region, came into view across the valley, 'uplifted in the likeness of a mighty throne, canopied by clouds, and approached by a giant staircase, each step of which is a precipice laden with eternal snow and trodden only by the chamois hunter' (Amelia). The crooked pyramid of the nearer Antelao, clear and distinct and now free of mist, loomed over my shoulder. It, too, was crusted with snow.

When I reached the Rifugio San Marco (open!) Sunday lunch was being served. First a glass of white wine and mineral water because I was thirsty, then spaghetti with lettuce from the garden. I had the pick of two bunk rooms, one narrow and dark, the other airy and bright, with a little window overlooking trees. No choice, really. I took the room with a view.

Five Italians impeccably turned out in stylish climbing gear (not much put to the test by the look of it) sat down to large platefuls of pasta. The fat one wore dainty plastic gaiters in red and white stripes. Gaiters in this weather, in the heat of the sun! I was scornful.

I left them still trenchering while I set off for a high valley, an amphitheatre of wasteland under jaggy peaks, and there I was alone again. To the left, pocked white steps rose towards the Sorapsis, a mountain only a shade lower than the Antelao. To the north, blocking the end of the valley, stretched a massive wall of bare rock, the Monte di Caccia Grande. Close by was the Tore di Sabbioni, a domed tower whose sheer sides were colour-stippled like a canyon in Colorado. A metal plate bolted to a boulder told that in 1877 the guide Luigi Cesaletti, climbing alone, was the first to scale the Tore, 'a milestone in the history of the Dolomites'.

With plenty of daylight left, I thought I'd search out the Slataper, a bivacca sited under the Sorapsis at a height of 2,600 metres. The route took me over successive terraces of rock and among huge boulders, and sometimes over patches of snow in which I sank over the ankles. The Italian's dandy gaiters might have been useful after all.

In all this delirium of rock and snow someone had been busy with a paintbrush. As usual the way had been liberally marked with red splotches, but I could see that many in this region had been obliterated, painted over with grey to match the colour of the stone.

I was nearly at the bivacca before I sighted it. It was perched just under the level of the pass, a bright yellow cabin, hardly more than a box, anchored by hawsers to the rock table on which it sat. I lifted the latch and stepped in. It was spotless. It was also surprisingly roomy. Nine bunks were fitted neatly three high against the walls, each with a pile of bedding folded on top. There were two wooden benches and a little folding table, a small window, and a first-aid box and two candles on a shelf. I reflected on its neat state compared to the condition of the average Scottish mountain bothy, filthy, broken down dens that so many of them are.

When I got back to the San Marco I found I had neighbours. Two Germans from Munich were sharing my room. Their gear was stacked tidily on the end of their beds, and they were padding about in stocking slippers. They showed me their route planned for the next fortnight, mostly along wooded ways, with the paths inked red on the map. They'd arrived that day at San Vito, having been driven through the Alps by their wives. On completion of the tour they'd phone home so that they could be collected the next day. It seemed an efficient arrangement. OK for those with wives.

By seven in the morning they were packed and ready to go. It was a perfect day. Setting out later, I wore shorts, packed a few essentials in a bumbag and took a new way that led over a hillside full of scree. On the narrow track across the stones I came face to face with a line of sheep. '*Scusi*', shouted the shepherd, anxious in case I scattered his flock, and I had to scramble above the track to let them file past.

Then the way was blocked by a large boulder on which someone had painted the word *difficile* in black letters, with an arrow pointing upwards. I scrabbled over it without too much difficulty and reached a sharp crest between two valleys. The valley ahead broadened into meadows and then forest as it fell away towards a river, beyond which rose a range of hills dominated by the Marmarole mountain, another of Amelia's favourites. Below me was a big grey rifugio with its shutters flung wide. There was washing on the line and I heard voices. But before investigating the rifugio I worked my way round the hill behind it in order to catch a glimpse of the far side of the Antelao and its grubby glacier. A burn fed by the meltwater came bounding down in a rocky defile.

I went back to the refuge, had a glass of white wine, bought postcards and had a long and inconclusive discussion with two girls at the counter, in which the one word we all recognised with certainty was *francoboli* – postage stamps.

I loitered on the walk back, sitting on a bluff to eat sandwiches with the Pelmo in view, in a necklace of puffy white clouds. Then back to the San Marco and the long descent to the main road to wait for a bus back to Calalzo. A mile and a half up the road was a farm building called the Dogana Vecchia, the old

custom house on the the former border line, where Amelia and L
had crossed from the new Italy of Mazzini and Victor Emmanuel
into the old Austrian empire. I ought to have walked on to look at
it but it was hot and I was tired. I just sat idly in the shade.

In Calalzo I gave the Hotel Ferrovia a miss. Somewhere
cheaper would do – and besides, would they remember my free
dinner and call me to account? I found a comfortable house where
I sluiced away the sweat and dirt of the hottest day. In the pizzeria
that night the clientele were glued to the TV watching football, and
in the airport at Mestre next day there was also a football presence,
two Scots fans in bedraggled kilts, mournful in defeat and hung
over. To Amelia all tourists (she, of course, was not a tourist but a
traveller) were barbarians. Whatever would she have thought of
football fans?

My last sight of the Dolomites was from the air; weird domes
and steeples that might have been designed by Gaudi, tinged with
the setting sun, an exotic fringe to the snowy Alps. Earthbound
Amelia had a more leisurely parting. She had a last relaxing week to
spend, still within sight of her mountains.

'As long as we can stroll out every evening to the old bridge
down behind the Cathedral and see the sunset crimsoning those
mighty precipices, we feel that we have not yet parted from them
wholly. They are our last Dolomites . . . we bid them farewell'.

16
Alive with the sound of Italiano

A friend has a flat in a village in the north of Italy, an hour by bus from Lake Como. I can sit on the balcony in the evening as the swifts swoop around the eaves and watch the setting sun colour the white limestone summit of the Grigna, the mountain opposite. Unseen behind me is the other considerable mountain of the district, the Pizzo di Tre Signori. Both are worth climbing.

Which first? By chance, the decision was delayed. On my first night in the village of Introbio I saw a flyposter on a wall in a lane just off the square. It had been put up by the local branch of the Italian Alpine Club to advertise an outing that weekend to Lago Brocan and the Rifugio Genova, with the possibility of an ascent of the Argentera. None of these names meant anything to me and I'd no idea where the Argentera was. But I found the club headquarters in a little upstairs room and signed on for the excursion.

The 'pullman' – standard Italian for a coach – set off at six in the morning with forty boisterous Italians on board including a toddler who would later, in the hills, be strapped to his father's back. It promised to be a hot weekend. Already the temperature was registering seventeen degrees, and even with the air-conditioning going full blast the pullman became stuffy in the course of a five-hour journey that took us via Milan, Turin and the hill town of Cuneo. We crossed wide rivers meandering sluggishly through grey mudflats and passed whole fields of tall sunflowers with their fringed heads turned in ranks towards the sun. Past the outskirts of Turin were vineyards in the foothills and signposts for towns whose names are on bottles, Asti, Cinzano and Barolo.

At midday we reached the mountain town of Entracque and combed its narrow streets for food and drink. For me, ham sandwiches and a litre of something cold, slightly fizzy and tasting vaguely familiar; it was labelled tea (actually, *te*) but had little in common with a good cuppa. A grinding ascent took us along leafy lanes never meant for a motor coach to the diga, or dam, on the calm blue lake of Chiotas, where we debussed.

The heat was blistering and the climb to the hut devilish in spite of partial shade from scattered shrubs and bushes. Sweat channelled down my face and I got shaky knees scrambling up a rocky bit where a rope was attached for help. I thought I was going well, all the same, until I saw our leader, a lean athlete with a ginger beard, loping effortlessly upwards with the aid of two sticks.

We came to a stony road blasted out of the cliffside, where a yellow digger was hoisting a roll of wire netting in its bucket jaws. Beside it, giving directions to the driver, was a man in shorts and a dented blue hard hat, with climbing kit jangling at his waist. Ropes dangled down from fixed points in the trees above, and round the next rock was a man fastened to the slope blasting away with a power drill. They were making the cutting safe, fixing nets to trap falling rocks. The scene put me in mind of Provence and the two mountaineering road-makers I'd shared a room with in St Martin.

The road stopped at a dam with a small lake behind it. Hidden just above was the even smaller Lago Brocan, whose turbulent outflow we crossed on a couple of tree trunks laid among the boulders. Water gushed underfoot. The lake lay in the bed of a narrow hanging valley littered with gigantic rocks and surrounded by bare peaks. Marmots shrieked from their stony dens and later we were to see chamois raising incautious heads (easy prey for hunters) on the skyline. Numerous white streams rattled downwards, fat with meltwater from the snowfields which still defied the summer sun.

Beside the lake, 2,000 metres above sea level, stood the two-storey Rifugio Genova. We arrived by twos and threes, dropping rucksacks at the door, stripping damp T-shirts from our sweaty backs and laying them out on flat rocks to dry.

A sudden storm brought me down from the attic room

where most of our party were to doss, matily more or less rubbing shoulders on jampacked mattresses, just in time to rescue my dry T-shirt from being soaked again. The heavy raindrops soon turned to bouncing hail. Then the thunder crunched and the lightning zizzed. When the storm had passed the birds piped up again, but it was still humid and oppressively hot.

We crowded into the dining room for plain food, pasta and stew. My neighbour at table urged me to eat up. '*Troppo magro*', she said.

Magro? – I looked it up in the pocket dictionary. Thin, skinny. Everybody laughed.

'*Scozzese?*' – Yes, I was Scottish.

Did I wear a kilt? – I said I hadn't the legs for a kilt. *Troppo magro*. More laughter.

Then, inevitably: What does a Scotsman wear under his kilt. I said I'd never looked.

As the meal progressed and the wine flowed the decibels rose alarmingly. Forty Italians were having a good time and you won't get noisier than that. They leapt to their feet, they shouted from table to table, they gestured extravagantly. There was uproar.

Sandwiched among us were a handful of others, not of our party, and these cowed unfortunates were dumbstruck. I talked to one of them, a Dutchman. Would a Dutch party make such a din? He looked up from his plate and his eyes were wide with wonder. 'It's impossible', he said with feeling.

Then they sang. Never such singing. Sad, sentimental songs, mostly, that sounded to me like traditional folksong until one emerged as Amazing Grace – which, I suppose, is traditional enough, though it's from another culture. They sang with passion, full voice, heart and soul. The women were especially fine; one or two with a hard-edged quality of voice, strong and true, that made me think of gypsy singing from eastern Europe. I could have listened all night, and willy-nilly, I nearly did. Tired, I took myself to the attic and tucked the rough blanket round me, and still some were singing, out of doors now, under the stars.

'*Andiamo, mangiare*'. Let's go. Breakfast.

Ginger Beard was shaking me awake. I followed him out,
creeping so as not to wake the others. It was five o'clock and still
dark.

Downstairs a small group of the elect were breaking bread
rolls into bowls of weak tea. They looked formidable, tough,
seasoned. One was Jack Palance to the life, big-boned, lantern
jawed, jutting nose; a character out of a Western (the
baddie). Others were hardy veterans with sinewy limbs and skin
like leather. There was a young lad, fit and robust, and one woman,
tough as nails, who barely deigned to look at me, and when she did
it was with a scornful glance. Or so I thought, rubbing sleep from
my eyes. This was clearly an elite. I realised that none of them had
slept with the rest of us in the attic. They'd spent the night in
sleeping bags in the basement among the boots and gear.

They looked up without greeting when I joined them, and
got on with eating. What had happened to the fun? It had
evaporated in the night. Faces were set. No one spoke.

And Franco wasn't there. Franco was still upstairs fast asleep.
This was disturbing because it was Franco who had invited me to
join this Argentera task force. Tall, black-bearded, with a little
English, Franco had been delegated the previous evening to broach
the subject of the Argentera with me. Would I care to join the
assault party?

Was it difficult? (my stock question).

'*Difficile?* What's difficult?' And Franco shrugged his shoulders.

Franco admitted, as far as I could understand, that there was
one iffy bit, a bad step where the route traversed an overhang.

'You look down and there's nothing below', he said. But
there was a fixed rope to cling to in case of need, he assured me.

I should have gone. I knew it then and I know it now. But as
I lay in the night thinking of the morning call, the bad step had
preyed on my mind. I have a poor head for heights. To look down
on a few hundred feet of nothing is a prospect too awful to
contemplate.

I looked round the table. The faces gave nothing away. These were hard men (and one hard woman). Was I out of my league? It would be shameful to hold them back — if they cared to hold back, which they might not. Would they just leave me if I lagged, or faltered on the edge of the abyss?

No one spoke English. Franco was unconscious upstairs. No one to talk to, no one to explain, no one to give a word of encouragement.

'You go on. I'll wait for the others', I said.

They rose, and went so silently I didn't hear them leave the hut. Fifteen minutes later when I went out to see where they'd got to, I couldn't spot them. A stambucco, a dark goat-like creature with great gnarled horns, was cropping the grass a few yards away. There was no other sign of life. The barren landscape had swallowed them up.

It was still early when we softies filed out. As we climbed a narrow track above the lake the Argentera lay behind us in the glare of the morning sun, bulky and bare of vegetation, seamed and patched with remnant snows. I scanned it with binoculars but still couldn't find the climbers. The Argentera is the highest peak in this mountainous border country between Italy and France and I looked back at it wistfully, regretting my loss of nerve. On the other hand, the route we took was no picnic. It was steep and rough, though mercifully in deep shade, and near the top there was a stretch of awkward rock to cross and two spreads of shelving snow which demanded a little care. This brought us on to the Colle di Fenestrelle (odd name — Pass of the Little Windows) beyond which, on a grassy platform hemmed in by rock slabs, we sat and ate, drank and sunbathed. It was still only 9.30 but it was hot already. A sign on a wooden stake gave the height of the pass as 2,463 metres, so we'd climbed more than 1,200 feet since setting out from the Genova.

At our feet was a glassy pond edged by snow, beyond which the hill dipped sharply into a grassy valley. Another large mountain, blue in the shadows, lay beyond. On our right the sun reflected off a wall of rock, a sliced-off side of a hill streaked with ochre.

A man with a bare beer belly now pulled a map out of his trouser pocket; not so much a map, really, more a menu. The paper napkins at table in the Genova had a rough sketch of the area printed on them, and this is what he now carefully unfolded and consulted. It's the first time I've witnessed navigation by napkin.

The fat man and two pals — one the oldest member of the party — started down the hill. The veteran, a wiry 79-year-old with a white toothbrush Adolf moustache, was dressed for the part in stout breeches, thick socks up to his knees, a serviceable shirt and a Tyrolean hat with a feather in it. He had a long wooden-shafted axe, a real antique, which he used as a walking stick. He was tough. He kept up a steady pace all day long, sometimes in the lead, never lagging. As this trio skirted the pond and passed out of sight over the lip of the hill, he hallooed, and his yodelling bounced of the rocks.

Down we went, sometimes picking our way through a wild garden of flowers. High among the rocky outcrops were nests of gentians and in the crevices tiny succulents grew. The grassy slopes were starred with many white and yellow flowers. In the valley bottom ran a clear, wide stream and close to it stood the Soria hut where six of us, including the elderly alpinist and one of the women singers, lunched on big platefuls of spaghetti. The Soria was an oasis. Unlike the Genova, which is a dedicated climbers' hut, the Soria serves a broader trade. Sunday walkers were tramping up the track from a distant road end, and others were scattered alongside the burn basking in the July sunshine.

From the Soria a broad stony track — *una strada*, a street, joked the singer — followed the stream down the valley. Cupped between the hills, the heat was intense and it was good at last to reach clusters of beech trees that offered shade. It was a long and thirsty walk. In a meadow a herd of brown cows gathered round a stone hut, flicking at flies with their tails, and a woman sat beside them alone with her thoughts. I saw the rearguard of our party crossing the meadow to buy milk from her.

We reached the road-end where cars were parked, and we must have looked like hoboes among the holiday families. My face was burning, my shirt was clinging to my back, my legs were muddy. The bad news was that we still had seven kilometres to walk along the motor road to meet the pullman and the Argentera climbers.

At Milan, at seven in the evening, a temperature gauge showed 32 degrees. Hot, hot. At night I sat on the balcony of the flat, tired, with a chill glass of white wine in my hand, watching the sun sink behind the Grigna. The sky was an angry red.

17

Bye-bye John

There followed a night of rain and rolling thunder, and in the morning the grass and shrubs were wet. The chestnut trees dripped on me and there was a soft tapping in the leaves overhead. I was on my way to the Pizzo di Tre Signori, taking a long way round that would bring me in good striking distance of it the next day.

Behind the piazza the narrow, winding lanes were confusing. The church clocks had still to strike seven and hardly anyone was about. An old man with a small black and white terrier hobbled out of a doorway and started to climb the cobbled steps between the houses, resting at every other step. He had a tall wicker basket on his back, empty except for a plastic bag with his piece in it and a bottle of *acqua minerale*. Where was he going? It seemed a shame that a frail old man should have a day's work to do. He stopped to talk to a woman neighbour (his knees were bad, he told her) and I passed by.

After a roadside saint in his wooden stall the lane became a track, still roughly cobbled and softened underfoot by the thin yellow catkins and boat-shaped leaves of the chestnuts. A notice on a tin plate nailed to a tree forbade the hunting of hares (open season for other species?). The track surmounted rocky outcrops on the verge of a wooded ravine and crossed a cascading burn by a humpy concrete bridge, then plunged into a dark forest of huge conifers. Brown needles carpeted the way, with lines of long cones lying on the ground like strings of turds. Wisps of mist in the dark foliage made it an eerie place, a gloomy natural cathedral. I was glad to break out into more open woodland of friendly broadleaf trees, where the sun was beginning to strike through the patterned foliage.

Soon I reached what a note on the map called the ancient beech tree (*vecchio faggio*); an old man (or woman maybe?) of the woods. It stood just under a ridge surrounded by its progeny, a monster in girth with seven boughs each as big as a mature tree springing from the parent stem. Centuries old (*centiale*), but still in rude health and luxuriant foliage.

It was hot by mid morning when I reached the Rifugio Buzzoni on a headland overlooking the Valsassina. Here I'd promised myself a cold drink, but contrary to the promise in the tourist literature the hut was shut. So I sat on a bench outside, spread the map in front of me and reflected on the next move while eating a dry sandwich.

Above the treeline is the Passo di Gandazzo, a broad lawn offering views into two green valleys, the Valsassina (where I'd come from) and the Valtorta. A thousand feet below in the Valtorta is a ski station where a few cars were parked. When I arrived at the pass two men and a boy who'd just come up from that direction were glumly contemplating a sign that told them the bad news about the Buzzoni hut. *Chiuso*, closed.

I continued upwards by a stony path, with the occasional brief scramble over barricades of rock. There was a chiming of running water, music to the hot and thirsty walker. I saw where a thin film of water moistened the rock nearby, and a few steps beyond I came to the spring from which it issued. Sparkling water arched from a thin pipe in a rocky niche, surrounded by a halo of wild flowers. A shiny tin mug was chained to the stone, and I drank deep from water so cold that the bottle I filled there remained chilled for hours, sunk deep in my pack.

Refreshed, I climbed on to the Passo di Toro, where the track twisted and turned over rocky spurs, offering dizzy views into the Valtorta. Where it's trickiest there's a chain bolted to the rock wall, which I disdained to touch – rather bravely, I thought, for a faint-heart like me. From there the sharp peak of the Tre Signori came suddenly into view. I could see where a route, just the merest thread, snaked up from the base of the beetling rock and then lost itself under the summit. It looked a challenge, but tomorrow I proposed to climb the peak by a different approach.

A mass of purple azalea clothed a green slope and then, approaching the Rifugio Grassi, a miniature forest of bushy alders. Their presence puzzled me. Alder is a water-loving tree associated in my mind with burn and loch. What was it doing on those parched heights?

I had no desire to linger at the Grassi. Two tubby Italians dressed for walking were stretched out sunning themselves.

'*Buongiorno*', I said civilly.

They eyed me coldly and did not reply.

Maledizione, then. A sort of sotto-voce sod you.

The Tre Signori lay immediately ahead, but I made a diversion. An ill-defined track led off the crest and had me scrambling over a succession of sharply tilted slabs, the last of which I had to straddle before finding a foothold on loose and flaky slate on the far side. Here I met a grizzled couple who shook hands and politely attempted to make sense of my shaky dictionary Italian. Was I German? (everyone assumed I was German). They seemed pleased to find a Scotsman. We agreed solemnly that the area was interesting, geologically speaking, and that the walking was good. We smiled a lot at each other. We gazed around and made expressive approving noises. Then we shook hands again and went separate ways, I down through debris towards the Lago di Sasso. Sasso means boulder and at the rim of this lochan stood a cluster of giant boulders, fragments torn from the cliffs above. Two anglers sharing a rod between them were trying their luck from these high stony platforms, but though I watched them for a while I saw nothing caught.

All the little lakes in this neighbourhood teem with trout and other fish. The Lago di Sasso is the smallest and the prettiest of them, a little gem on middle ground between two landscapes. Behind it rises a chain of rocky, snow-gullied mountains dominated by the Tre Signori, and before it curves the broad pastoral valley of the Biandino.

At the head of this valley were byres with a herd of brown cows standing amid a clangour of bells. Half a mile down a dusty

road was my resting place for the night, the refuge Madonna della
Neve (Madonna of the Snow), a small stone house with a chapel
and bell tower adjacent, a scene of pilgrimage. In 1836 the people
of the Valsassina were spared from the plague and ever since they
have given thanks for deliverance. Every August thousands march
singing from the valleys below for a service round the stone altar in
the field by the chapel.

A large man with brown corduroy trousers yanked over his
paunch was sitting outside in a deckchair reading his newspaper. He
lifted his specs at my approach and announced that he was the
priest. Half an hour later, when I'd stowed my gear in a tiny upstairs
room and taken a shower, I walked out and heard a low droning
issuing from the open doors of the chapel. The dim interior was lit
by two candles and by their light I saw the Father standing at the
altar with a surplice over his shirt and cords. He was intoning a
service to a congregation of three; the woman of the house, her
daughter and little grandson William (not Guglielmo, the Italian
equivalent). The reason for this English name, pronounced Weelyum, was never explained and I was left to speculate.

At dinner that evening the Father switched on the TV and
became emotionally involved over Italy v Nigeria in the World Cup
(it was 1994). Eyes glued to the fuzzy screen, he bayed dissent and
boomed approval in a loud bass voice.

I was the only guest that night so I had the choice of the four
bunks in a poky room wedged at the top of a wooden staircase. I
stretched out on a top bunk with the outline of a wooded ridge in
view through a small square of open window.

When I rose in the morning the priest was sitting at table, still
reading his paper. Laid on the table beside him was a long stout
stick. After breakfast I started to climb to the top of the ridge by a
sandy path, and when I looked back at the Madonna from half way
up, I was surprised to see the stout Father far below, stepping out
after me with a wide-brimmed hat on his head and the pilgrim staff
in his hand. I thought I'd be sure to shake him off but whenever I
turned he was still in sight, plodding in my footsteps.

Once I reached the top of the escarpment there were two ways to go. I discussed routes over coffee with the warden of the Santa Rita hut, which looks over the Biandino valley. I could keep to the crest, dodging over the uptilted slabs that formed a serrated skyline of unknown challenge, or I could make a detour to the base of the mountain via a track known as the Sentiero della Tempestada, which I think must mean the path of the storms. I chose the latter and followed the faint track of the Tempestada down through groves of shrubby alder into a corrie full of jumbled rock, with a black dome of mountain hanging over it. The weather, fine at the start of the day, had taken a turn for the worse. Clouds were rolling in, mist was gathering on the peaks, and a stiff breeze had sprung up.

A helicopter came chuntering down the valley, swinging wide to clear pylons and power lines. It settled on a knoll close to a stone hut and three men got out, ducking below the blades. Ten minutes later the machine returned to deposit four more. I watched them through the glass from my perch on a rock and wondered what they were up to. Climbers stealing a march on time? If so, they were remarkably light on gear.

I followed a stream upwards and emerged in a desert of sounding stones and slaty rubble, below which lay the Lago dell'Inferno, the infernal lake, on whose cobalt surface floated islets of glistening snow. The lake was deep, dark and dammed (if not damned) by a barrage, from which power lines swooped into the valley. A curtain of mountain ringed the lake, extending from a madness of fantastic rock spires to the bare, broad shoulder of the mist-shrouded Tre Signori. Now and again the mist parted to reveal a speck of a cross on its summit. White water rushed over a precipice, the sound of it magnified in the amphitheatre.

Suddenly I heard voices. Looking up, I saw a party of school children in jazzy clothes breasting the col above me, having reached it from the other side. As I trudged upwards they streamed down past me and later, on the col, I met a solitary walker in a yellow T-shirt. He assured me the route to the top was straightforward.

Difficile? – No. Absolutely no exposure, which was what I wanted to hear. Follow the signs. It was marked all the way with red daubs on the rock and the number seven. He produced a bag of chocolate chip biscuits and we munched together before he made off down the way I'd come.

I became aware of dim figures advancing in the greyness above. Here and there were patches of snow to cross, but mostly there was bare rock underfoot, slab after slab, and then a level stretch before the last rise to the misty top. On my left there were precipitous drops into the dark blue lake – a nasty shock if you were to miss the way. Beside a rock someone had left a bunch of fresh flowers at a plaque in memory of 'one who loved the mountains'. I looked at the dates. He was 21 when he died.

Out of the gloom above my head came floating a babble of voices. I pulled myself over the last awkward shelf and discovered the source, a group of children who acted like a reception committee. As I appeared they broke into cheers, which is the first time I've had a round of applause on reaching a summit. What a happy hilltop.

There was no view, of course, all blotted out by the weather. It's said to be wonderful. The Tre Signori – the three lords – in question refer to the three provinces whose boundaries meet at this 2,553-metre point, but all I could see was the immediate circle of bare rock patched with mossy vegetation, and crowned with a big metal cross round which the school party posed for photographs.

They were a breakaway group from the main party I'd met earlier. The leader was an athletic-looking type in a Club Alpino T-shirt, and among the adults there was also a nun with trainers peeping below her long white skirts. I wondered if she hitched up her skirts to scale the rocks. Or had she wings and did she fly?

It was chilly and I didn't stay long. I left ahead of the youngsters, but after I'd lingered on the slaty pass watching the helicopter retrieve its passengers, they came into sight behind me, and shouts of 'Bye-bye John' echoed down the valley. I stopped for a breather at the Santa Rita and was offered a sip or two from a bowl of black coffee laced with grenadine. It was dynamite. There they told me that the helicopter had been ferrying a TV crew who were making a film in the area. Then in poured the whole school party and there was instant hubbub. I left to another round of ciaos, cheerios and bye-byes.

Only Weelyum's mother at the ironing board was in sight when I passed the Madonna della Neve, so I never learned if the stout father had made it all the way up to the Santa Rita that morning. The long walk home took me down a rubbly road in a forest valley. There were birds I'd never seen before in the underbrush, brown splashed with black, white and blue, large as jackdaws and with a rasping call. At the bottom, beside a bridge, was a memorial to soldiers of the Rosseli Brigade who'd fought and died *'in questa valle su questa strada'* – in this valley on this road, a simple and moving phrase. Twelve names, and growing below them in a hollow log, a tuft of flowers.

Two days later I rose early to attempt the Grigna. The bullnosed mountain was shrouded in cloud which peeled back fitfully, suggesting the weather might clear. It was not yet six. To start the ascent I had to walk from Introbio to the neighbouring village of Pasturo (which means what it looks like, pasture). At the top of the village old houses in flaking ochre and terracotta were jammed together, with a little church in a square from which a cobbled cart track led upwards through woodland of chestnut and beech. The path soon narrowed and degenerated, with vegetation encroaching and stones displaced, the common fate of abandoned bridle tracks. Small sloping fields were newly mown, and behind the isolated farm houses I was aware of a roadway snaking about in the neighbourhood. Occasionally I heard a car or the put-put of a moped as people went to work.

After two hours of steady ascent the trees thinned and vistas opened up, and I reached two or three buildings at the edge of a pond, where the only signs of life were a few cattle and a hen or

two scrabbling in the dirt. Just beyond was a small refuge, the last
habitation and a welcome staging post on the route to the top. The
Rifugio Pialeral (since then demolished, I hear, by an avalanche)
had a dark little dining room where two buxom women in black
dresses were shelling peas in preparation for lunch. *Oggi gnocchi,*
gnocchi today, said the varnished board made from a slice of tree
hanging outside. The refuge had bunks for a dozen and seemed like
a good place to stay, with its cosy atmosphere and fine view over
the valley, but I paused only for a buongiorno, a beer and a chat in
my basic and broken Italian before continuing.

The hill rose ahead, a solid barrier of limestone gleaming in
the sun, veined by bands of hardy vegetation. On the southern side
it dipped to a col before rising again in a ragged ridge that led to
the sister peak, the craggy Grignetta or Grigna Meridionale. On the
col is a bivacca, a concrete shelter where it would be fine to sit and
eat lunch if it weren't for the wildlife, a few long-horned shaggy
mountain goats which have acquired a taste for sandwiches. Not
caring to be pestered by greedy beasts I passed on without pause to
the sharp ridge which led straight to the top. Down below lay the
eastern reach of Lake Como, glimpsed occasionally through thin
scudding mists. The bare rock, darkened and polished by the
passage of boots, continued along a corniche from which rocky
spurs plunged dramatically towards the lake. Here and there the soft
stone was scratched and gouged by winter crampons.

A number of walkers were strung out along the ridge. I
passed one from whose pack stuck an aerial, thinking he might be a
local mountain rescuer, until I realised that the voices coming
through the static were some Saturday morning Italian radio
show. A bit thick. Keep the ether clean! I distanced myself from the
crackle as fast as I could.

A building, round which small figures were clustered, capped
the ridge. This, to my surprise, marked the summit. The Brioschi
hut sits slap on top of the mountain, a gross intrusion by man
against nature. I admit that it must be awesome to spend a night up
there in the Brioschi. Imagine it in the eye of a storm with the roof

groaning and creaking, the floor trembling and the world torn in pieces below.

For the present there was sunshine and drifting banks of white cloud, and views to every far horizon. I sat on limestone rubble underneath the glass chapel which abuts the Brisochi (heavenly views, every prayer a picture) and gazed down at hardy souls arriving by another and more arduous route. A chain anchored in the rock helped some to scale the last sloping shelf.

I hadn't a map for the far side of the hill and decided not to attempt it, which proved a wise decision. I later discovered that I might easily have strayed off the route, more than likely ending up at Lake Como. So after lazing in the sunshine for half an hour I returned the way I'd come. In all it had taken less than four hours from Pasturo to the top, which was good going and impressed the two fat ladies when I called at the Pialeral for a drink.

'To the top and back? You've been quick'. Such words are always flattering to hear. By this time the place was crowded. Families were sitting on the verandah having lunch. I guess most of them had come by road.

Cocks crowed, cows lowed and the smell of new-mown hay was heavy in the air. I came out of trees and crossed a bend of the road, meaning to plunge into the woodland track on the other side, when a red 4x4 appeared and the driver hailed me. Did I want a lift? I accepted gladly, without a shade of guilt, and arrived back at the flat at barely three o'clock in the afternoon. A happy man. There was beer in the fridge and a good book to read.

Sunday, my last walking day, I spent pottering about in the neighbourhood of the Zucconi Campelli, a Dolomite-like peak whose name I thought had a Scottish ring about it (but no Campbells in these mountains). Pottering is not strictly accurate, for before I reached an alp-like plain called the Bobbio I had a two-hour uphill slog in broiling morning sunshine, partially shaded but never cooled by the surrounding forest.

It was silent among the trees except for my footfalls on the zigzag forest road. Behind me, when the cover broke, I could see the distant Grigna lit by the early sun. For most of the time I was plodding along on my own. Two jeeps rattled past in a haze of exhaust fumes near the start, and three walkers overtook me near the top. A girl in skimpy black shorts and top, with thighs the colour of varnished log, strode past like a lithe amazon. A tap-tapping announced the next walker, a young man swinging along with the aid of two ski sticks. Last came a swarthy middle-aged man, lean and wiry, with a red cap on his head.

Had I known, I'd have taken the ski lift that operates from the next village, Barzio, but I'd assumed it would be closed after the spring season. To my chagrin, as I neared the top, I heard it whirring up and down, whisking summer strollers to the Bobbio. Families with picnics were debarking from the gondolas and spreading over the plain, where most were content to remain. Hardier excursionists were heading for the surrounding heights.

From a vantage point above the green bowl of the Bobbio I was rewarded with a view of the whole Valssasina, with a corner of Lake Como just visible in the hazy distance and a cluster of red roofs indicating a lakeside town. There was a full circumference of hills, with the Grigna dominant in one quarter, tipped with a wisp of cloud but otherwise bathed in sunshine. On the other side of the Valsassina rose the tortured Pizzo di Tre Signori, and on the far horizons were ranks of other showy, snowy peaks. I walked up bouldery slopes among crags and cliffs, hauling myself through a funnel of scoured rock to reach a minor peak. Opposite me, and quite close, were the Dolomite-shaped spires, pinnacles and sugar loaf formations of the Campelli, forming a rugged screen silhouetted in a thin grey mist. Two climbers were strung out on a rock face, and matchstick figures dotted the several crests. Their chatter wafted across the divide.

I made a rough translation of a note on the map: 'The eastern summit can be reached by a route which is rather dangerous and the view doesn't reward the effort'. Well, I thought, why quarrel with that? A spot of danger and a poor lookout did not appeal to me at that moment. I beat a retreat.

There was a cable car waiting at the ski station but the weather was fine, I was feeling fit, it was still early, and I could see a track traversing wooded slopes to the Passo di Gandazzo, where I'd paused five days before on my trip to the Tre Signori. I turned my back on swifter locomotion and set off towards the Gandazzo. On a tumble of coarse, iron-red scree, whom should I meet but my brown-limbed morning amazon, striding still. We nodded and passed.

I sat on the grass at the Gandazzo, where several paths meet and a number of people were about. Up came a fat man of sixty or more in baggy breeches, one leg flapping loose down his calf. Stopping for a breather, he rummaged in his pack and took out a long red water bottle wrapped in a knitted cosy (for insulation, I suppose, like an old-fashioned hot water bottle cover) and took a slug from it. Then he handed it to a small boy nearby who was whining at his mother: 'Mummy, I'm thirsty'. The fat man surveyed the scene contentedly, mopped his brow, peeled off his thick jerkin and moved on.

On my descent I passed the Buzzoni hut, now open and lively with people. I hadn't intended to stop.

'Hi John, come here!' someone bellowed from a top window.

I looked up. Framed in the window was a black-bearded face, a face I remembered from the Argentera trip. So I turned aside, had a beer or two, and spent a jolly hour with Franco and his wife and friends.